HERS
UM
ER

Farm
ear Bristol
822862

SYMONDS'
HAYMAKER
CIDER

SYMONDS' CIDER
& ENGLISH WINE CO.
Cider & Perry Mills, Stoke Lacy,
Herefordshire.

GW00671920

DUNKERTONS
PERRY

DUNKERTONS CIDER CO.
HEREFORDSHIRE.
TEL. PEMBRIDGE 653

4.55
LITRES
(1 Gal.)

TRADITIONAL CIDERS AND PERRY

TAUNTON

EXHIBITION
STRONG DRY STILL
CIDER

MADE BY THE TAUNTON CIDER CO. LTD.
NORTON FITZWARREN · SOMERSET · ENGLAND

2 litres
NO DEPOSIT – NO RETURN

ESTABLISHED 1728

ASPALL CYDER

ASPALL HALL, SUFFOLK

MADE FROM ORGANICALLY GROWN APPLES WITH NO TOXIC OR
CHEMICAL SPRAYS AND NO ADDED CHEMICALS OR PRESERVATIVES

1 litre
35.2 fl oz.

ONS
NAL
DRY
ER

NO
RETURN

HEREFORDSHIRE ENGLAND

fl oz

Y IN OAK VATS

ury

ROUGH NORFOLK

Countryman

SCRUMPY

Full Strength
Still
Farm Cider

4·8 litres

COUNTRYMAN
CIDER

FELLDOWNHEAD
MILTON ABBOT
DEVON

REGISTERED TRADE MARK

TO BE CONSUMED WITHIN 48 HOURS OF OPENING

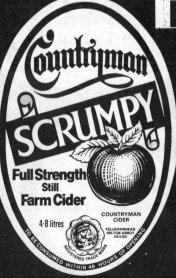

Bland's
West Country

Real
CIDER

Dry

In nineteen seventy – one Vernon Bland decided that real
cider was going the way of real ale – annihilated by its
mass- produced industrialised counterpart. So he started
to make the real farmhouse cider once more – no added
flavouring or gases, just the true traditional full-strength
cider.
Pressed, fermented and matured at
Blands. West-End Lane, Oldbury-On-Severn, Avon

1 litre

Contains permitted preservatives.

Good Cider

by the same author
JAMS, PICKLES AND CHUTNEYS
BREADLINES
THE VEGETABLE GROWER'S CALENDAR
IN SEARCH OF FOOD:
traditional eating and drinking in Britain

Good Cider

DAVID MABEY

WHITTET BOOKS

First published 1984

© 1984 by David Mabey
Whittet Books Ltd, 113 Westbourne Grove, London W2 4UP
Design by Paul Minns
All rights reserved

British Library Cataloguing in Publication Data
Mabey, David
 Good cider.
 1. Cider
 I. Title
 641.2'3   TP563

ISBN 0–905483–34–0

Printed in Great Britain at The Pitman Press, Bath

CONTENTS

Acknowledgments

A great many people have assisted me during the writing of this book. Top of the list are the cider-makers, large and small, who have willingly provided help, information and inspiration. Their names all appear later in the book.

I should also like to thank the National Association of Cider Makers, the Long Ashton Research Station and the Museum of Cider, Hereford, for their co-operation.

Finally, I should give due acknowledgment to Anthony Gibson's pioneering cider column in the CAMRA newspaper, *What's Brewing*, from 1978–81, which provided me with a great many valuable leads.

1
THE STORY OF CIDER

✦

CIDER has been part of English life for almost a thousand years. It has been drunk by rich and poor; its virtues have been extolled by doctors and physicians; it has served as an item of trade, as wages and as a political weapon; no other drink has been endowed with such magic and power.

EARLY DAYS

No one knows when cider was first made. Although there is evidence that apples have been cultivated for at least 3,000 years, there is no record of when our inquisitive ancestors first turned the juice of the apple into an alcoholic drink. In Britain it was probably the Celts who found little crab apple trees growing wild in hedgerows and made the fruit into a liquor resembling cider. The crab apple was too hard to bite and too sour to eat, but once it had been crushed and its sharp, acidic juice had been allowed to ferment, it was transformed. But the Celts weren't great cider-drinkers; mead was their favourite and they also brewed a kind of beer from barley.

The word 'cider' comes from the ancient Hebrew *cekar* or *shekar*, meaning 'strong drink'. When the Romans arrived in Britain, they brought with them a word from the same source, *sicera*. They ate apples, knew about orchards and introduced many new strains into this country: Palladius, writing in the 4th century AD, lists 24 varieties. They don't seem to have made cider, since their great love was wine and they practised viticulture widely in the fertile regions of lowland Britain.

The Anglo-Saxons also knew about apples, tended their *aeppel-tuns* (orchards) and drank *aeppel-win*, which was probably a form of rough unsweetened cider; however, they seem to have preferred mead and beer.

THE FRENCH CONNECTION

It was a different story in France, where both cider and perry (made from wild pears) were drunk a great deal, particularly by the poor. It is recorded that brave St Guenole, living in Brittany in the 5th century, chose to chastise himself by living on a diet of water and perry; others, with even stronger constitutions, existed on perry alone. Punishment indeed, considering perry's devastating reputation as a purgative!

North-west France was renowned for its apples and orchards; its geography, soil and climate made it much more suitable for apples than grapes. So, while the rest of France made wine, Normandy made cider. And when the Normans set foot on English soil in 1066, they were anxious to transplant their cider-making skills.

There were already apple orchards in south-east England in the 11th century, and Kent and Sussex became the first cider-making counties. The Benedictine monks of Battle Abbey, dedicated in 1094, were some of the first to acquire the taste for cider and it must have cheered their lives greatly. After that, the habit spread quickly: new orchards were planted right across southern England, down through Wiltshire and Dorset into the West Country, north into East Anglia and Lincolnshire, and through Buckinghamshire into Gloucester, Hereford and Worcester. There were even plantations as far north as Staffordshire and Yorkshire. New varieties of apple were imported from France and trees were taken by ship from ports on the Kent coast to Bristol, where they were used to build up the West Country orchards. And with the trees came the skills of cider-making, as well as new techniques for milling and pressing.

One of the earliest apples to come into use was the 'pearmain', and 'wine of pearmains' (a synonym for cider) was mentioned as early as 1205, when it formed part of a rent paid by the manor of Runham in Norfolk. Despite these new varieties, wild crab apples still found their way into the cider mill: in 1296, one Simon de Monte was fined in Wakefield because he failed to gather crab apples for the lord of the manor, who was thereby deprived of two hogsheads of cider.

A DETOUR INTO THE KITCHEN

As cultivated apples were used more and more for cider, most wild crab apples were made into 'verjuice', a valuable asset to the medieval cook. It was made in a similar fashion to cider, as this old account shows: 'Gather crabbs as soon as the kernels turn blacke, and lay them in a heap to sweat and take them into troughs and crush with beetles (heavy wooden mallets). Make a bagge of coarse hair-cloth and fill it with the crabbes, and presse and run the liquor into Hogsheads.' (Quoted in *Food in England*, Dorothy Hartley)

Verjuice was a basic ingredient of the highly spiced sauces that were such a feature of cooking in the Middle Ages. With parsley, grapes, egg yolks and garlic, it made a sauce for roast goose, while for preserving fish it was combined with saffron and nutmegs to make a thin yellow broth. It was also used for pickling vegetables and remained popular until Elizabethan times, when it was gradually superseded by vinegar and lemon juice.

GARDENS AND IMPROVEMENT

By the beginning of the 14th century cider had definitely arrived; it was now the common drink of the people, often overtaking ale in many areas. And when demand outstripped supply, casks of the precious brew had to be imported from France to quench the collective English thirst.

But the 14th century also saw the beginning of the Hundred Years War, which dragged on until 1453. One effect of this conflict with France was that supplies of superior French wine – traditionally the favourite tipple of the English aristocracy – were cut off, and the gentry were forced to sample locally produced beverages. Cider was a revelation, and many felt it could compete with the best wine.

By now, cider was a commodity, an article of trade that could be stored and transported without any problem; it was also much safer to drink than the highly polluted 'fresh' water supply. (This no doubt led to the practice of baptizing babies in cider rather than water.)

But for all its virtues, cider was still a cottage industry, based more on trial and error than on sound knowledge or skill. The first necessity in improving the quality of cider was to improve the raw material, the apples themselves. Gardening and fruit growing became all the rage in the 16th century, and people like Richard Harris, fruiterer to Henry VIII, were quick to see the problem: 'The plants our ancestors have brought out of Normandy had lost their native verdure.' So he imported new grafts from France and the Low Countries and laid out extensive orchards at Newgardens, Teynham, in Kent. Many others followed suit, and soon the 'garden of England' was blooming.

The fruit-growers of Kent and Sussex were lucky because they could send their produce to London quickly, so they concentrated on soft, perishable dessert fruit, including eating apples. In remote parts of the West Country, however, roads were terrible, and it was fruitless trying to send produce to London for sale. So the growers in these parts dedicated themselves to cider-apple orchards. The resultant cider was strictly for local consumption at first, but it was a start; the West Country cider industry was under way.

4

SCUDAMORE'S SKILFUL HAND

By the middle of the 17th century there were around 350 different varieties of cider apple, with a whole vocabulary of colourful, rustic names: Slack-my-girdle, Sheep's Nose, Rubystreak, Foxwhelp, Rusticoats and Handsome Maud to name but a few.

The time was ripe for the appearance of cider's first champion, the young Lord Scudamore. Tired of the fickle pleasures of life at Charles I's court, he returned to his estates at Kentchurch in Herefordshire and there indulged his great passion for growing apples and making cider. He experimented with planting and grafting and, under his lead, the whole of Herefordshire became one vast apple orchard. He also bred the greatest of all cider apples, the Redstreak. The juice of this celebrated apple was unequalled for making cider: it was a perfect blend of harshness, sweetness and astringency. No wonder it was celebrated by cider poet John Philips, whose epic of 1708 entitled 'Cyder' made it clear that the Redstreak was:

> *Of no Regard 'till Scudamore's skilful hand*
> *Improv'd her, and by Courtly Discipline*
> *Taught her the savage Nature to forget:*
> *Hence styl'd the Scudamorean Plant.*

Scudamore's other master-stroke was the introduction of bottled cider. Until the 17th century, cider had always been served directly from the cask, and it was often improved by spicing. In *A New Orchard and Garden*, William Lawson had noted that 'if you hang a pocket full of cloves, cinnamon, ginger, and pills of lemon in the midst of the vessel it will make it as wholesome and as pleasant as wine'. However, Scudamore's friend Sir Robert Mansell, who was owner of the glass trade monopoly in England,

5

tipped him off about the increasing habit of bottling in the wine trade. The advantages of bottling ciders were obvious: it could withstand the rigours of long journeys over bumpy un-made roads, and the very process of bottling would help to preserve it.

Scudamore also spent long hours blending and fortifying (adding spirits to) ciders by storing them in old sherry casks. When the cider was put into bottles and left to mature, it quietly fermented and the resulting drink was clear, bright and spark-ling. It was the champagne of the age. Indeed it was often passed off as true champagne by unscrupulous bootleggers. Addison (obviously not a cider fan) attacked these 'spurious wines' in one of his essays in *The Spectator*, claiming that the purveyors were 'by the power of magical drugs raising under the streets of London the choicest products of the hills and valleys of France, squeezing Bordeaux out of sloes and drawing champagne from apples'.

Inspired by the sophistication and style of this fine cider, Scudamore also set the fashion for drinking it out of elegant and beautifully engraved glasses rather than the cumbersome pottery mugs that served for the working man's rough cider.

GOLDEN DAYS

The upsurge of interest also resulted in the first books about cider. Following John Evelyn's *Pomona* of 1664, which also contained articles by Dr John Beale, Sir Paul Neil, John New-burgh, Captain Sylas Taylor and other cider enthusiasts of the day, John Worlidge of Petersfield in Hampshire published *Vine-tum Britannicum* in 1676. It was cider's first classic, described as 'A Treatise of Cider and other Wines and Drinks extracted from Fruits Growing in this Kingdom'. It also contained 'A Descrip-tion of the New-Invented *Ingenio* or Mill for the more expedi-tious making of Cider'.

6

Vinetum Britannicum:
OR A
TREATISE
OF
CIDER;

And other Wines and Drinks extracted from Fruits Growing in this Kingdom.

With the Method of Propagating all sorts of Vinous FRUIT-TREES.

And a DESCRIPTION of the New-Invented INGENIO or MILL, For the more expeditious making of *CIDER.*

And also the right way of making METHEGLIN and BIRCH-WINE.

The Second Impreſſion, much Enlarged.

To which is added, A Diſcourſe teaching the beſt way of Improving BEES.

With Copper Plates.

By *J. Worlidge.* Gent.

LONDON,

Printed for *Thomas Dring,* over againſt the Inner-Temple-gate; and *Thomas Burrel,* at the Golden-ball under St *Dunſtan's* Church in *Fleet-ſtreet.* 1678.

7

This was a real breakthrough. Until then, cider apples had been laboriously crushed and ground using stone mills driven by horse-power or the brute strength of a man. Worlidge's rotary mill was much more efficient and paved the way for all later devices in the field.

These were golden days for cider. Subtle and different blends were produced for the connoisseur alongside the robust farm-house cider. And it was no longer just for local consumption: after travelling the whole country in the 1720s, Daniel Defoe concluded that cider was one of Devon's redeeming features because 'they have so vast of quantity of fruit, and so much cider made, that sometimes they have sent ten, or twenty thousand hogshead of it in a year to London, and at a very reasonable rate too.' It wasn't only Londoners who craved for cider: the 'gentry and yeomanry' of the north of England also loved it and even preferred it to wine.

Cider went to sea and was popular with sailors, not only because it was alcoholic, but because it was safer than drinking water *and* prevented scurvy (the seaman's scourge – a disease caused by a deficiency of vitamin C). By 1800, cider was being prescribed for 'vomiting, gout, ailments of the urinary tract and rheumatic diseases'; it was also 'an effective and cleansing surgical dressing'.

THE TAXMAN COMETH

The Long Parliament of 1643 levied a tax of 1/3d per hogshead of cider on retailers, but it was more than a century before the taxman set his sights on cider-*makers*. The year was 1763 and the Seven Years War had just ended; the government was short of cash so Lord Bute decided to turn his legislative guns on the cider-makers, and levied a tax of 4/- per hogshead.

The cider-makers knew this was bound to happen, and mounted a propaganda campaign with slogans like 'Let the cider tree, From tax be free', and they had the words 'No Excise' engraved on fine cider glasses. But to no avail. The dreaded day arrived, and was marked by some mournful demonstrations. This was the scene at Ledbury, as reported by the local paper:

> A procession was made through the principal parts of this town by servants of the cider merchants . . . the day the Cyder Act took place . . . in the following manner viz. a man with a drum covered with black crepe beating the dead march, drumsticks reverted, two mutes with crepe hat bands and black cloaks and empty barrels upon a bier carried by six poor farmers dressed in cyder hair clothes; the bells rung muffled all day and every face expressed a sympathetic sorrow for the impending ruin that awaits the country.*

But the cider-makers weren't prepared for the tactics of the Excise Officers who, for the first time, were given the power to raid houses in search of dutiable goods. It was a spectacle that angered the public and politicians alike and inspired William Pitt the Elder to quote the famous phrase 'An Englishman's home is his castle' when opposing this law. In a few years it was gone, although the original tax on retailers remained until Lord Wellington's administration in 1830. (The latest duty on cider was introduced with the Finance Act of 1976, when it joined beer, and wine and spirits as a taxable brew.)

PAYMENT IN KIND

Even in the 18th century, cider-making was still a job for farmers and farmers' wives and it was common practice to pay labourers at least some of their wages in cider, rather than hard cash. Farmers who had a reputation for making good potent cider had

* Reproduced in *A Taste of Cider* by Shirley Harrison (David & Charles, 1982)

little difficulty in getting workers to help them out, especially during the busy seasons of hay-making and harvesting. The practice was known as 'truck', and the cider dished out to the men was often very weak, made from second pressings of the fruit and called 'ciderkin' or 'purr'. So it's easy to understand that a large amount was consumed.

Workers were normally given three or four pints a day, although during hay-making this was increased to two gallons by some farmers. Although labourers were used to the stuff and could generally hold their drink, there are many stories of drunkenness and of workers becoming addicted. The practice of paying in kind was finally outlawed in 1877 by the Truck Acts, which were pushed through partly by the Victorian temperance organizations who demanded that the workers be paid in cash (or 'dry cider', as it was known).

Even so, the practice did continue in many parts, and daily rations of cider were still being handed out to workers in the 1930s, as old photographs of men with their horn cider mugs and 'costrels' (miniature wooden casks) show quite clearly.

MODERN TIMES

Cider went through a bad patch in the early years of the 19th century. Cider-makers began to feel the pinch from the taxman and as the wheels of the Industrial Revolution started to turn, there was more competition from other drinks. The brewing industry was becoming organized and beer had the advantage that it could be made throughout the year; gin had become the opium of the people, especially those doomed to a wretched life in the new cities; and as roads and transport improved, wine from the Continent started to reappear and fill up the cellars of the rich. By the 1880s there was also a general depression in agriculture, and cider orchards were neglected as farmers turned their minds to ways of producing more beef and grain for the ever-growing population.

But all was not lost. Indeed the Industrial Revolution created a surge of interest in science and technology that took cider out of the hands of the farmer and into the factory. Machinery and technical processes were improved and made more efficient, the work of Louis Pasteur and others helped to give cider-makers an understanding of the way yeasts and fermentation worked, and the development of the railways meant that producers in the once-remote West Country and Herefordshire now had access to ready markets in the big cities.

In 1870, William Gaymer turned his small cider-making business in Attleborough, Norfolk, into a large scale commercial enterprise. A few years later, over in Hereford, Henry Bulmer founded what was to become the world's largest cider company. Many others followed suit. At the turn of the century, cider found a new champion, C.W. Radcliffe Cooke, who was MP for Much Marcle in Hereford. He spoke out in favour of cider at every possible opportunity, and became affectionately known as the MP for Cider! In 1903 he was partly responsible for setting up the National Fruit and Cider Institute, which was founded to bring science to cider. This eventually merged into the highly regarded Long Ashton Research Station, allied to the University of Bristol, which has pioneered many developments in cider-making, and with the East Malling Research Station, Kent (founded in 1913) has made great strides with the breeding and cultivation of apples.

By the 1960s, the image of cider was beginning to change. The old traditional farmhouse 'scrumpy' was still made in small quantities in the West Country by a few devotees, but its image was still rustic, not to say rusty. The large cider-making factories were turning their attention to producing a drink that was fashionable, appealing and completely standardized. Like their colleagues in the brewing industry, they were convinced that keg was the answer. They began to filter, pasteurize and carbonate their cider and pack it into pressurized metal containers or 'kegs' so that it would keep almost indefinitely.

As it turned out, traditional cider was simply waiting for a well-timed revival. And help was to come from an unlikely source. The cider advertisers had done their work well and keg cider was increasing in popularity at the expense of the traditional brew. But in 1973 the Campaign for Real Ale (CAMRA) was founded to promote real, traditional beer. Over the past ten years it has been impressively successful in changing both public tastes and the attitudes of the brewers. There has been an enormous swing back to traditional beer, and in the wake of that success, traditional cider has found a new lease of life. New cider-makers are starting up, and those that have clung on over the years now find that business is booming. It's exciting news for everyone who loves good cider.

2
THE CRAFT OF
CIDER-MAKING

Lo! For thee my mill
Now grinds choice apples
And British vats o'erflow
With generous cider
                    (John Philips, 1708)

IT sounds simple, even miraculous. Choice apples ground in a mill to produce an abundance of cider. Of course that isn't the whole story; cider-making isn't quite as simple as that.

At its best, traditional cider is pure fermented juice with nothing added: no sugar, no extra yeast, not even water. Briefly, the process is as follows: ripe, good quality cider apples are harvested and then crushed in a mill (at this stage different varieties of apple can be blended); the crushed fruit is pressed to extract the juice, which is put into casks and allowed to ferment naturally, with no added yeast, so that the sugar in the fruit is converted into alcohol. After about four months the cider can be racked off into another cask and is ready for drinking.

This is the ideal method, and hardened purists would say it is the *only* way to make true traditional cider. In practice however, most cider-makers bend the rules. They may use dessert apples, or indeed any apples they can lay their hands on: cider apples can be scarce, and it's often a choice between making cider from what fruit is available or not making it at all; sugar may be added to sweeten the cider; the juice from different batches of fruit may be blended after pressing; water may be added to dilute the cider and reduce its alcoholic content from around 8% to 3% or 4%, the legal minimum. Sometimes extra sugar and yeast is added in the cask to 'condition' the cider, to create a secondary fermentation and give the drink a slight sparkle.

These practices aren't traditional, but for reasons of economics and convenience they *do* happen. What is needed is a code of excellence by which cider can be judged; cider-makers using the traditional method should be given every encouragement, but the fact that other cider-makers add a little sugar or water shouldn't necessarily be an outright condemnation of their products.

It's a very different story with the cider-making giants, who have, until very recently, been committed to producing a bland, uniform cider that will satisfy everyone and astonish no one. They need vast amounts of fruit, which comes from many sources – they have often been accused of using reject dessert and eating apples as well as imported concentrated apple juice from abroad. Back in 1977, the *Sunday Times* suggested that up to 80% of the apples used by one major company came from France, while another was importing quantities of fruit from Tasmania.

The apples are stored in huge silos, washed and passed on to sophisticated electrically powered mills which reduce them to pulp; the pulp is then transferred to hydraulic presses, where the juice is extracted. At this stage sodium sulphite is added to kill off the natural yeast in the juice, and a special yeast is added to produce a controlled fermentation. Once fermentation is complete, after about four weeks, the cider is drained off and transferred to vats to mature. Then it is usually diluted with water to reduce its alcoholic content; it may also be sweetened. The contents of different vats, made at different times from different batches of apples, are blended to produce a cider with the required qualities.

If nothing more is done to the cider, except perhaps the

addition of extra sugar and yeast once it has been put in the cask, it is often sold as traditional draught cider. However, if it is destined to become one of the big, nationally advertised 'keg' ciders, it will subsequently be pasteurized, carbonated with fizzy CO_2, coloured and filtered so that it is perfectly clear and sparkling.

These products are 'cider' in name only, and to be fair most of them are pleasantly innocuous. They are the cider-makers' answer to keg beer, nothing like the real thing, but they are consistent and absolutely reliable. Drinkers from the south of England to the north of Scotland know what to expect when they order a pint.

Whatever the outcome, the business of cider-making always starts with apples. And that's where we begin.

Apples

Pick a cider apple from the tree and you will see that it is a small, hard fruit with a heavily blotched skin. Bite into it and you will again notice its hardness; then after a deceptive moment of sweetness, the apple literally turns sour. The taste becomes intensely bitter. It dries the mouth. It is impossible to eat. All of this testifies to an ancient connection with the wild crab apple.

VARIETIES OLD AND NEW

The Romans were enthusiastic apple growers and could boast some twenty different named varieties, but it wasn't until the 13th and 14th centuries that specific varieties of cider apple were recorded. Two which have stood the test of time, and can be found growing even today, are the legendary Genet Moyle and the Cap of Liberty. Genet Moyle was thought to be extinct, but a single tree has been discovered in Herefordshire and this, it seems, can be propagated by simply sticking a twig or branch into the soil.

More and more varieties began to appear in the 16th century, and by the end of the 17th century there were some 350 different types growing in England. These were the great cider apples of the past, with an extraordinary selection of names: some like the Redsteak, Rubystreak and Leathercoat were purely descriptive; others, like the Kingston Black and the Eggleton Styre, commemorate the places where they were first found or cultivated; then there were the tantalizing varieties . . . Foxwhelp, Oaken pin, Bloody Butcher, French Longtail, Coccagee, Cat's Heads, Handsome Maud, Slack-my-girdle.

But the natural life of a cider apple tree is at most 150 years, so it was important to experiment, cross existing varieties and seek out wild crab apples that could be taken into cultivation. In fact most of today's cider apples were unknown before 1900 and have been specifically bred for the purpose. But the names still have a colourful ring – Brown Snout, Yarlington Mill, Chisel Jersey.

Variety and change is part of the business of agriculture, with old-established names being replaced by new breeds over the years. But there's now tremendous economic and political pressure to influence the food we grow and eat – and that includes apples. Competition from abroad is forcing English apple-growers to fight back, so government and bodies like the Apple and Pear Development Council are actively encouraging farmers to grow only certain varieties of apple. Uproot your interesting trees, they say, and replace them with a few commercially desirable varieties. Forget the traditions and history behind your apples and concentrate on the profit. The end result will be fewer varieties, not only of eating and cooking apples, but of cider apples as well.

TYPES OF CIDER APPLE

It's almost impossible to define the perfect cider apple, but a good one will have a unique and delicate balance of three elements: sugar, acid and tannin. The sugar produces the alcohol, the acid gives a sharpness and the tannin a complicated blend of roughness, bitterness and astringency. Every variety of apple has a different composition, different proportions of these valuable constituents, but for convenience they have been divided into four categories.

Sweets: These are low in both acid and tannin, and produce a bland, soft cider with no great qualities. 'Sweets' are used mainly to tone down the stronger elements in other types of apple, which would be too powerful on their own. The most common variety is the Sweet Coppin; Court Royal was a favourite in the past, but is rare today.

Sharps: These are very high in acid, very low in tannin. Some varieties of cooking apple have the same qualities and are often used in place of true cider 'sharps' such as Crimson King and Brown's Apple.

Bittersharps: These are fairly high in both acid and tannin. Many of the favourite cider apples of the past, like Foxwhelp, Joeby Crab and Skryme's Kernel were 'bittersharps', but they have fallen out of favour because they are less versatile than 'bittersweets' (see below). Most dessert apples, e.g. Bramleys, fall into the 'bittersharp' category; however the increase in price and reduction in quantities of these dessert varieties may yet result in a renewal of interest in cider 'bittersharps'. Two that are still going strong are Kingston Black and Stoke Red.

Bittersweets: These are low in acid, high in tannin and give today's West Country cider its characteristic qualities. They are liked because they are versatile, they can be blended with ease and subtlety and because they produce cider which is to the liking of today's drinkers; it is smoother, less sharp and less astringent than the ciders of the past. The balance of acid and tannin is such that no other apples need to be added to make a good, drinkable cider, although 'sweets' and 'sharps' *are* used to create different blends.

The best 'bittersweets' are late-ripening varieties like Dabinett, Yarlington Mill, Tremlett's Bitter, Chisel Jersey, Brown Snout and Fillbarrel.

West Country cider-makers believe that only true cider apples will make good cider, and certainly their products are very distinctive. Some varieties like the legendary Kingston Black are used on their own to produce fine cider. But most favour a blend of different varieties to give different types of cider. It rather depends what fruit they are growing or can lay their hands on, but the blending can be quite complicated, involving numerous varieties chosen to give the correct balance between acid, tannin and sweetness.

In the south-east, things are very different. There's no tradition of growing cider apples, but a great history of cultivating dessert fruit like Bramleys. And cider-makers in this part of the country use culinary and dessert fruit to produce cider that is generally much more 'fruity' and sweeter. It may be different, but only a purist would dismiss it out of hand.

Orchards

Cider apple trees are not particularly fussy and will grow almost anywhere. But they do prefer a warm, moderate climate, not too

cold, not too windy and with plenty of sunshine. Ideally orchards are planted on south-facing slopes sheltered from strong winds which could damage the trees and blow down the fruit before it was ripe. The trees will also grow in most kinds of soil, but they prefer places where the soil is warm and light; they also like to 'keep their feet dry', so it is best to avoid damp places.

Apple orchards in full blossom are one of the glorious sights of the English countryside. Until quite recently the orchards were planted with fine trees which grew 20–30ft tall with a tangled canopy of branches that hung heavy with fruit as autumn arrived. Because of their size and spread they had to be planted some 30ft apart, with a maximum of 40 trees per acre; but the space between the trees wasn't wasted because it was used for grazing. Often it was necessary to protect the trees, and back in the 17th century John Evelyn described how trees were planted on little mounds surrounded by prickly bushes and a ditch to keep cattle at bay. (Curiously, one of the greatest of all cider apples, the 17th century Redstreak, was more like a dwarf tree and was planted intensively with only about 16ft between each tree. Because of this the whole orchard had to be enclosed with a fence to keep out livestock.)

Harvesting apples from these orchards was an awkward process; the trees took something like 15 years to come to a full fruiting, and could only produce 2–3 tons per acre. This didn't suit the commercial growers *or* cider-makers who were demanding more and more fruit as the cider-drinking habit spread. The old 'standard' trees took up far too much space, they were inconvenient, uneconomical and inefficient at producing fruit. So whole orchards were uprooted and replaced with squat 'bush' trees.

The idea was to plant intensively, cramming up to 240 trees into each acre. These new bush trees were fruiting after about 3 years and at their peak after 8 or 10, and it was hoped that they would yield as much as 10 tons of fruit per acre: the heaviest crop in the smallest space. The trees were also convenient to harvest by machine.

Despite this the cider apple harvest has become more and more erratic. Some years there is almost none at all and vast quantities of apples have to be imported. Because of the increasingly unpredictable English climate, the trees rarely fruit to their full capacity, in fact if conditions are bad the bush trees are no more productive than the old 'standards'.

Nowadays most cider apple orchards are confined to the west of England, in Devon, Cornwall, Somerset, Avon, Gloucester, Hereford and Worcester. In south and east England (Kent, Sussex, Norfolk and Suffolk) cider is made from local dessert fruit, and its character is very different. But none the worse for that.

PESTS

Pests and diseases are a fact of agricultural life, and plant breeders are always striving to produce disease-resistant varieties. This is certainly true of apples, and growers are also armed with an arsenal of potent pesticides to spray trees and fruit at different times of the year.

Attacks come from caterpillars, apple aphids, apple suckers and red spider mites as well as from fungal diseases. The growers in their turn hit back with BHC, DDT, malathion, dimethoate and the like. Despite reassurances that these sprays are used correctly, it is nevertheless a disquieting thought that apples are being treated in this way. No wonder that cider-makers now wash their fruit before milling it – something that never happened in the past. Although spraying is now widespread, it's heartening to hear of growers going against the trend. John Chevallier Guild, who grows apples and makes cider at Aspall Hall, in Suffolk, is one of the few who produces his crop organically.

Gathering the fruit

Harvesting cider apples is an autumnal trade that occurs at the 'black end of the year', from early October to late November. For hundreds of years it was simply a matter of allowing the fruit to ripen and letting it fall from the trees naturally. It was a rare sight to see workers actually picking cider apples, although they often used long ash poles to knock down the fruit.

Sacks full of apples were gathered up and made into heaps or 'tumps' which were covered with straw. Fruit picked early in the season had to be dealt with and milled quickly; the later, harder varieties could be left to stand until after the New Year. The purpose of this was to mature the fruit, to allow it to lose some moisture and concentrate its sweetness and flavour.

Naturally this method of harvesting was fine when there was not a great deal of fruit and there were plenty of helping hands to do the gathering. But as the old orchards were replaced with row upon row of bush trees, so mechanical harvesters moved in. These are now able to glide systematically between the rows shaking the fruit to the ground, sweeping it up and collecting it. Because the apples are easily bruised and damaged by the machinery, they have to be milled and pressed soon after harvesting.

Large cider-makers handle vast quantities of fruit (Bulmers deal with some 50,000 tons in a season). The apples are stored in huge silos, then washed by being passed through water. All the debris sinks to the bottom and the good apples float.

Milling

Cider apples are hard and consequently have to be crushed before the juice can be extracted. Before technology came to the cider-maker's assistance, this had to be done by hand, and the apples were pounded or 'stamped' with a hefty piece of wood or a mallet. It was a long, laborious process, but it did work, and it was still common practice on Devon farms as late as the 18th century, when it was claimed that two men could between them crush 20–30 bushels of apples in a day using long handled mallets and a trough made from a hollowed-out tree trunk.

Mechanization of the process came not from England, but from the Mediterranean and the Middle East, where stone mills had been used for centuries to crush olives. During the European Renaissance, similar machines were devised to deal with woad and other dye-stuffs, linseed, charcoal (for gunpowder) and metallic ores. And by the end of the 16th century the idea of

Fig. 8. Cider. Mill.

*The design of an 18th-century horse-drawn mill
(without the horse).*

using a stone mill to crush apples had spread across the English
Channel from France and was being put to use in the cider-
making regions of the West Country. Although designs varied
according to area, the principle of these mills was always the
same: a heavy stone wheel, set vertically and attached to a
massive central post was drawn round a stone trough, crushing
the fruit in the process. Some mills, a few feet in diameter, could
be drawn by the cider-maker himself; other monsters, up to 14ft
across, needed horse-power.

The horse was harnessed to the yoke attached to the central
post, and then the long, tedious business of grinding could
begin. Apples were piled on the central pier around the post and
as the horse plodded round, the ciderman followed, knocking
fruit into the trough with a stick. When these had been crushed
he threw in a couple of buckets of water to prevent the mill from
clogging up. Then more apples went in and the grinding continued, as man followed horse round and round, both getting
wearier by the hour. By the end the pulp was almost spilling over
the sides of the trough.

Cider-making, an idyllic view.

The crushed pulp or 'must' – a dark brown, strong-smelling mess – had to be just the right consistency, and it was the ciderman's job to judge when it was ready for the next stage, pressing. If it was too coarse it would not press well; if it was too soft and runny it would be unmanageable.

Once installed, these stone mills were a permanent feature of West Country farms, and farmers were naturally reluctant to give them up and move over to other, more efficient methods. But change did come, and at the beginning of the 19th century farmers in Devon and Somerset began to experiment with a different kind of mill, designed back in the 1670s by John Worlidge. This was the 'Ingenio'. Based on the principle of a Cuban sugar mill, it was a rotary device in which the fruit was passed through a hopper and chewed up by the wooden teeth of a cylindrical roller. The first mills of this type needed manual labour, but they were much quicker than stone mills and had the advantage that they could be powered by an engine. As designs improved during Victorian times, these mechanical 'scratter'

*Two version of John Worlidge's 'Ingenio' cider mill,
the model for all later types.*

mills were able to crush several tons of fruit in an hour. Today's cider-makers still use mills of this kind, although they are now powered by electricity and stainless steel knives chop and pulp the fruit.

Pressing

Once the fruit had been milled, the pulp was ready for pressing, the all-important process of extracting the juice. The designs of the presses themselves were ingenious, although most were based on the designs of wine presses used on the Continent. There were also many regional variations. In Devon and Somerset, the common method was to spread the apple pulp onto barley straw, which helped to bind it together while it was being pressed. Alternate layers of pulp and straw were put on to make a large sandwich or 'cheese' which was then fitted into the press. As the massive oak headblock of the press came into contact with the 'cheese', juice began to run out, even before any pressure was applied by turning the screw. As more pressure was applied, more juice ran out. (While the aim was to extract as much juice as possible, the first juice – obtained without pressure – was considered to make the most exquisite and highly valued cider, and was often separated from the rest.)

Cider-makers in Herefordshire used a slightly different method. The technique here was to pack the apple pulp into horsehair cloths which were folded and built up into a cheese for pressing. It sounds easy, but in fact needed great skill to ensure that the whole edifice was stable and in no danger of collapsing.

In the eastern counties of England, cider-makers often used a kind of box to contain the pulp (sometimes mixed with straw). This was because the pulp from dessert apples used in that part of the country is notoriously slippery and difficult to manage without some sort of container.

Working a man-sized cider press.

The first juice, which poured out spontaneously, was thick, opaque, brown and very sweet; the very last drops were different – thin, pale, clear and almost completely lacking in sugar and natural yeast. Much of the cider-maker's skill lay in balancing the different qualities of these various pressings to get the best result.

In recent years, new methods of pressing have been evolved, which require less time and less work. The hydraulic Bucher-Meyer press from Switzerland is popular with large cider-makers but also with smaller firms like Sheppy's and Aspall too. The pulp is pumped into a cylinder containing a hydraulically operated piston which applies pressure and forces the juice out. The cylinder can be rotated and the pulp pressed again until no more juice can be extracted. The press can handle up to five tons of pulp in an hour.

The dry pulp or 'pomace' left over after pressing has always been put to good use. In the past it was often fed to pigs and chickens, although if it was a day or two old and had begun to ferment it must have caused a lot of animal drunkenness down on the farm! These days it is used as cattle feed and fertilizer and is a valuable source of pectin, an important gelling agent in jam-making.

Fermentation

This is the core of cider-making, the conversion of the sugar in the apple juice to alcohol. Traditionally this was achieved quite naturally without adding anything to the juice, which was put into corked wooden casks after pressing and simply left to 'work'. After a day or so a brown froth would begin to gather at the bunghole of the cask, and if the cider-maker put his ear to it he could hear the brew 'singing'. Depending on the weather and the temperature, the cask would be left to ferment for a couple of weeks if it was very warm, or up to two months in colder conditions.

Sometimes pieces of meat, perhaps a hunk of bacon or mutton, would be put into the cask, and this has given rise to exaggerated stories about rats in the casks and so on. A handful of earth or wheat might be thrown in as well. The aim of this was to get the cider working and to produce a good fermentation.

Cider-makers didn't know why fermentation occurred or why adding meaty tit-bits to the cask would improve the process. The answer, of course, was yeast. Traditional cider fermented naturally because yeast was actually present in the cask. For a long time it was thought that the yeasts were present on the apples, but now it seems that they come from the soil in the orchard, from the straw in the presses and from cloths and racks that come into contact with the cider. Adding meat to the cask provided extra nutrients for the yeast and thus helped fermentation; handfuls of wheat or barley provided starch which could be converted to sugar and then alcohol, while the habit of actually adding soil was a way of adding more natural yeast to the brew.

All of this was fine, but it was an unpredictable process that could not be controlled. The change came before the First World War when Dr Durham, an expert on yeast cultures and Bulmer's first master cider-maker, succeeded in isolating two wild yeasts that were responsible for fermentation. From then on it was possible to control the process, a development that suited the commercial cider-makers who were seeking ways of making a consistent good quality cider.

These days, large commercial cider-makers pump the pressed apple juice into huge fermenting vessels, originally made of wood but now made of concrete or mild steel lined with acid-resistant resins. The natural yeasts are killed off by sulphiting and a selected strain of yeast is added to produce a carefully controlled fermentation. The process usually takes 2–4 weeks, by which time all the sugar has been converted to alcohol and the resulting cider is very dry. The advantage of this is that the cider won't be susceptible to bacteria which could turn it sour; it allows the cider to remain in good condition for up to a year. This is vital since large cider-makers must be able to supply cider all year round, even though the actual process of cider-making is strictly seasonal.

Maturing

Once the cider has been allowed to ferment, the final stage of the process is maturing, which produces a mellow, full flavour. Farm cider-makers simply store their cider in casks which are sealed to keep out the air. On a commercial scale, the fermented cider is pumped or racked off, leaving the yeast deposit at the bottom of the fermenting vessels. It is then stored in huge vats. Oak was the traditional material for these, and some cider-makers still use huge wooden vats. (Bulmers have 130 of these – some capable of storing 60,000 gallons at a time.) Once the cider is in the vats, it can be tasted and blended to produce different ciders with different qualities.

Cider isn't matured for as long as wine, and most commercial cider-makers reckon it is ready for sale a few weeks after fermentation has ceased.

3
TYPES OF
CIDER

DRAUGHT CIDER

By definition this is cider that is 'drawn' from a cask of some kind.
It can either be dispensed by gravity, that is from a tap in the cask
which allows the cider to pour out naturally, or by means of a
handpump – as draught beer is served in pubs.

Draught cider is produced by broadly traditional methods,
although some cider-makers adhere more rigidly to the traditions
than others. At its purest, cider should be fermented apple juice,
made from English cider apples with no water or sugar added,
and it should be fermented without any extra yeast.

The word 'cider' originally meant 'strong drink', and the best
still lives up to its name. Real cider is about 8% alcohol by
volume, a few vintage brews are even stronger than that, but
most is now diluted to bring it down to about 4% – on a par with a
typical draught beer.

Traditional draught cider is always sold unfiltered, so it
appears cloudy in the glass. Some cider-makers are in the habit of
conditioning their cider by adding extra sugar and yeast to the
cask. This creates a secondary fermentation and gives the cider a
sparkle. The cider can be classed as 'dry', 'medium' or 'sweet'
depending on how it has been blended.

Like beer, draught cider needs a landlord who understands his
cellar and is prepared to look after it with care. Cider is a living
brew that is sensitive to the temperature and atmosphere, and it
won't keep indefinitely. So it needs to be sold in a pub where
there is a regular demand, otherwise it will turn sour and
vinegary in the cask.

*Harvest time in the fields. A farm worker with his
costrel of cider.*

A number of small farmhouse cider-makers still use wooden
casks, although the larger firms long ago abandoned them in
favour of metal ones which are easier to handle and clean.
Draught cider is also sold from little plastic barrels which can be
put on the top of a bar counter.

KEG CIDER

At present keg ciders like Bulmers Strongbow and Taunton
Blackthorn lead the field; they have – with the advertisers' help –
turned cider into a fashionable drink. Like keg beer, keg cider is
highly processed; it is pasteurized, chilled, filtered and put into
pressurized metal containers (called 'kegs').

To the marketing men it has all the virtues of cider and none of

32

its drawbacks; it is intended to be everything that traditional cider is not – clear, bright, sweet and fizzy. And it is absolutely consistent. Suddenly it has caught on in a big way, although it is really no more than a pale shadow of the real thing. But every drink has its day, and with the recent revival in traditional cider, the scales could easily tip the other way.

Keg cider is dispensed with the help of a cylinder of carbon dioxide, which forces the cider through the pipes and into the glass. On its way it usually passes through a cooler, so it comes out cool, like lager.

BOTTLED CIDER

Cider has been put in bottles since the 17th century and has been going strong ever since. In fact, for most people, bottled cider was the first cider they ever tasted (Bulmer's Woodpecker was every young girl's favourite drink at parties), but now the market is beginning to shrink. Most bottled cider is now simply keg cider packaged in a different way, but there are still a few high-quality bottled *still* ciders that are well worth sampling, e.g. Sheppy's Gold Medal Farmhouse Cider and Bulmer's No. 7 (to my mind the most interesting cider they produce).

One recent development is the appearance of low-carbohydrate bottled ciders such as Gaymer's Lite, which are intended to appeal to the slimmers of this world because they are very low in sugar.

Bottled cider will keep for a couple of years, provided it is unopened and is kept cool, at 45°–50°F (8°–10°C). Once opened it should be drunk straight away, as it quickly goes flat. Like lager, most bottled cider is best when chilled.

Pomagne, sparkling 'champagne' cider in champagne-style bottles with a cork, should not be kept more than 18 months unopened, as it can be affected by air in the headspace at the top of the bottle.

VINTAGE CIDER

The word 'vintage' is the source of great confusion among cider-makers. It can refer to the fact that the cider has – like wine – been made purely from fruit of one crop or harvest; it can also be used to mean cider which has been aged or matured for a long time, and it is even bandied about by advertisers and marketing men because it has an evocative ring; it is a tag that sells cider.

Cider-makers are always looking at new ways of presenting their brews, and one idea much in favour now is the 'bag-in-box'. This has already been used widely for beer and wine, although it has been criticized because the drink in the bag tends to deteriorate very quickly. Even so, it's an idea that appeals to large firms like Bulmer's and smaller enterprises such as Merrydown. And at least one farm cider-maker, Hills of Staverton, Devon, are considering the idea.

4
CIDER-MAKING
AT HOME

IF you have a taste for cider, it's well worth trying to make your own, especially if you have access to a good supply of fruit. Apart from some means of crushing and pressing the apples no special equipment is required, and the process doesn't involve the complicated techniques of the amateur wine-maker.

What follows is a general guide to making cider the traditional way, by crushing the fruit, extracting the juice and allowing it to ferment naturally without any added yeast. You will need to experiment and adapt the directions to suit your needs, but that is part of the fun.

Choosing the fruit

Ideally cider should be made from a blend of true bittersweet cider apples (see page 18), but in practice most people will have to make do with a mixed bag of unidentified varieties. Windfalls are excellent, and if you have friends who also have apple trees you can collaborate and pool your resources. Alternatively, make contact with a local fruit farmer, who may be prepared to put by some useful, if not top-grade, apples. To give you some idea how many apples you will need, you will get about 1 gallon of cider from 15–20lbs of fruit, depending on the type and the efficiency of your pressing.

If you know the names of the apples and their different qualities you can blend them to suit your taste; if you are simply using unknown varieties, then you have to work in the dark, so to speak. Bittersweet apples such as Yarlington Mill, Chisel Jersey and Brown Snout can be used on their own to produce excellent cider. Wild crab apples are also ideal. Sharp, acidic dessert varieties such as Bramley Seedlings and Tom Putts can be used on their own, but are best blended with some sweet varieties to give a more palatable cider. Sweet eating apples such as Cox's Orange Pippins, Quarrendon, James Grieve, Charles Ross, Crispin, etc., are useful when blended with other sharper varieties.

The actual blending of varieties is a matter of experiment, but you can start off with a mixture of equal parts bittersweet, sharp and sweet apples, and work from there. If you are aiming for a very dry, tangy cider, use 2 parts sharp apples along with 1 part bittersweet and 1 part sweet. If you prefer a sweeter, smoother cider, reverse the proportions and use 2 parts sweet apples to 1 part sharp and 1 part bittersweet. By juggling with the proportions you can obtain a blend that produces exactly the type of cider that you want.

Extracting the juice

This is the hardest and most strenuous part of cider-making: it is no mean feat to extract the juice from, say, a hundredweight of hard fruit, so any mechanical assistance you can dream up will be an advantage. Make sure the fruit is fully ripe before you start and cut out any serious bruises or blemishes. (In practice, this may not be essential; certainly no farm cider-maker would waste his time sorting through all his fruit.)

If you have to do it all by hand, see if you can enlist some help to lighten the load. Chop the apples roughly and pack them in batches into a wooden trough, plastic bin or large ceramic bowl – anything, in fact, that is not made of corrosive metal which will

The title page of John Worlidge's classic book,
Vinetum Britannicum *(1676)*

be attacked by the acid in the fruit. Crush the apples by pulverizing them with a heavy piece of wood or a mallet, until you have a coarse but quite solid pulp.

You can make use of domestic mincers and electric food processors, although these can only handle very small quantities of fruit at a time.

Pressing

This requires some ingenuity. The idea is to extract as much juice as possible from the pulp, with as little physical effort as possible. Home-brew and wine-making shops often sell small presses which are equally useful for grapes or apple pulp. Alternatively you can construct some device out of wooden blocks, perhaps levered down with a car-jack. Or you can pack the pulp into a cleaned and boiled hessian or nylon sack and pass it through a domestic mangle, making sure that you have a plastic or wooden container beneath to catch the flood of juice. It is important to completely fold over the end of the sack so that none of the pulp can leak out during pressing. You may need to make two extractions to get all the juice out of the pulp.

Fermentation

Next, transfer the apple juice to a large fermenting bin or plastic dustbin, depending on the amount you have. Cover the bin closely and put in a warm, dark place at 60°–70°F (15°–20°C) to allow fermentation to begin. It does so spontaneously, and often quite violently for a few days. Keep a close watch on it and remove scum as it forms. When it begins to subside and the first fermentation is complete, transfer the cider to gallon glass jars (suitably cleaned), fill up, and fit each with a cork and a

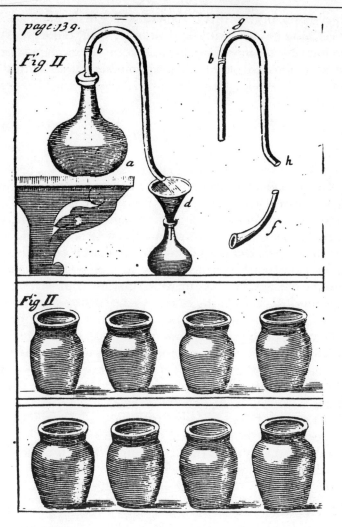

John Worlidge's way of racking cider by siphoning it from a glass fermenting vessel using a bent glass tube. This separated the clear cider from the lees or sediment.

fermentation lock, so that carbon dioxide can escape but no air can get in. The cider will continue to ferment, quite quickly at first, but later at a more leisurely pace as the remaining sugars are converted into alcohol. Keep the jars in a warm place during this time.

Storing and maturing

After a few weeks, depending on the conditions and the temperament of the cider, fermentation will be almost complete, with only the occasional bubble rising from the jars. You can then remove the fermentation lock, cork the containers and store them in a cool place for two to three months at least.

Or you can transfer the cider to pint or quart bottles. Use only beer or cider bottles: wine bottles are not strong enough to withstand the internal pressure which may occur when fermentation is finished. Siphon the cider into the bottles, which should be filled up to the neck. Old screw tops and rubber rings are excellent stoppers, or you can use plastic snap closures or metal crown tops (in which case a crimping tool has to be used as well).

If you want to give the cider a little extra sweetness and sparkle, add a teaspoon of sugar to every pint when you are bottling.

Don't expect the cider to become completely clear. The high pectin content of the apples and the fact that the cider has been fermented naturally mean that it will remain slightly cloudy even after it has been stored for a few months.

Once you have opened a jar or bottle, the cider needs to be drunk quickly (within 24–48 hours) but this is seldom a problem!

5
THE
CIDER-MAKERS

CIDER is booming and it's a rosy time for most cider-makers. While sales of bottled cider are continuing to fall, there has been a tremendous increase in bulk sales – particularly to pubs – since 1980, and the total cider market in the UK is now worth over £100m a year.

Sales over the last five years have shot up dramatically as these figures show:

> 1978. 46   million gallons
> 1979. 47   million gallons
> 1980. . . . . .46.5 million gallons
> 1981. 49   million gallons
> 1982. 60   million gallons
> 1983. 70   million gallons (estimated)

Much of this is due to the aggressive marketing and heavy promotion of keg ciders like Bulmer's Strongbow, Taunton Blackthorn and Gaymer's Olde English. (Strongbow alone is sold in more than 12,000 outlets.) Recently there's been a revival of interest in traditional draught cider, in the wake of the 'real ale' campaign, and this is certain to grow. While the cider market is tiny compared with beer (for every pint of cider, we drink more than 30 of beer), the prospects look very good for cider-makers big and small.

Three cider giants dominate the market, and between them

account for something like 97% of sales. Biggest of all is the family firm of H.P.Bulmer, which has 50%–60%; the Taunton Cider Company (owned by a consortium of brewers including Bass, Courage, Guinness, Scottish & Newcastle, Greene King, Vaux, Hall & Woodhouse and Wadworth) and Coates Gaymers (owned by Allied Breweries) have just over 20% each.

Competing in a fairly leisurely fashion for the remaining 3% are a number of small, independent cider-makers, with established products and an established market of their own. They are quite happy to tick over on a commercial scale without embarking on massive expansion or attempting to compete with the giants. Among them are names like Weston's, Merrydown, Symonds' and Aspall Cyder.

There are also scores of farmhouse cider-makers dotted around the country, particularly in the south-west. They use purely traditional methods, but don't make enough cider to warrant advertising. Some do sell it from the farm door and put up little signs on the roadside, but they are generally a secretive breed who shun publicity.

The cider boom has also spawned a number of new cider-makers who have started up in the hope of making some quick money. Many of these 'cowboys' are known to buy up quantities of cider from large producers, re-label and sell it as their own. Others simply produce second-rate brew from poor quality apples and pass it off as the best traditional cider.

The following list gives details of all the major cider-makers and their products, plus the names of the best farmhouse producers. Of course cider drinkers in search of the unknown are likely to track down many others.

The initials NACM after the names of some cider-makers indicates that they are members of the National Association of Cider Makers, an organization which meets to discuss and plan research and development into cider and considers topics like price, sales, etc.

Cider-makers given the 🍎 symbol are those who are producing cider by purely traditional methods using English apples and allowing the cider to ferment naturally without the addition of yeast, sugar or water.

Some ciders are awarded the 🍺 tankard symbol. These, in my view, are the best around, or at least the most interesting for one reason or another. I realize that cider connoisseurs are bound to have their own favourite brews, but this symbol should help to point newcomers in the right direction.

H.P. BULMER plc (NACM)
Plough Lane, Hereford, Hereford & Worcester
Hereford (0432) 276411

Founded in 1887, when Percy Bulmer, son of the vicar of Credenhill, Hereford, started pressing apples from his father's orchard. In his first year, Percy made 4,000 gallons of cider; today Bulmer's is the world's largest manufacturer, producing around 30 million gallons, over half the cider drunk in the UK each year.

Bulmer's produce a wide range of draught, keg and bottled ciders, which are widely available in thousands of outlets throughout the UK, from Cornwall to Scotland.

Visitors are welcome to look round the cider works, but it's advisable to book an appointment.

Traditional Draught: A cask-conditioned draught cider with a slight sparkle. Available dry, medium or sweet.

℗ *West Country Draught:* A traditional draught cider which is produced without secondary fermentation or conditioning, and is completely still. Available dry, medium or sweet. Limited to a relatively small number of outlets in the West Country.

Strongbow: A strong, dry, keg cider launched in 1960 and now one of the major brand leaders in the country. Also available in bottles and cans.

Woodpecker: First produced in 1896, and Bulmer's best-known cider. It is light and medium sweet and sold bottled and in keg; a dry version is also available in bottles only.

Special Reserve: A finely blended table cider with a little perry added. Available dry or medium-sweet in bottles or in the new 'bag-in-box'.

℗ *Number 7:* Bulmer's oldest brand, first made early in the 1890s. It is a light, still, extra dry cider produced exclusively from bittersweet apples and obtainable in half-pint bottles with a distinctive label depicting the Goddess Pomona.

Pomagne: A sparkling cider sold in corked, champagne bottles. Available dry or sweet. There is also a Pomagne Perry.

In addition to these brands, Bulmers also produce a number of regional variations like Gold Label (GL) sold around Hereford, Gloucester and Worcester; also Bulmer's Original, specially produced for the north-east.

🍎 🍐 J.M. CHEVALLIER GUILD (NACM)
The Cyder House, Aspall Hall, Stowmarket, Suffolk
Debenham (0728) 860510

Aspall Hall was acquired by the Chevallier family in 1702 who have been growing apples and making cider since 1728. They have some 60 acres of organically maintained orchards which supply the fruit for their products.

Aspall cider is sold in a number of pubs, wine bars and wholefood restaurants mainly in East Anglia and London.

Aspall Cyder: A range of ciders produced in the traditional manner. Available in bottles or flagons in three blends: still medium sweet, still dry and still extra dry.

Also noted for apple juice, cider vinegar and wine vinegar.

COATES GAYMERS LTD (NACM)
Kilver Street, Shepton Mallet, Somerset
Shepton Mallet (0749) 4224

Norfolk farmer Robert Gaymer started making cider in the village of Banham in the middle of the 18th century, but it was his great-grandson William who started the firm of Gaymers as a commercial enterprise in 1870. When he died in 1936, the traditions were continued by his descendants. Meanwhile, in 1925, Redvers Coate had set up a small cider-making factory at Nailsea in Somerset, and in 1956 this became a subsidiary of Showerings. Later, in 1968, the traditions of Norfolk and Somerset cider-making were merged, at the same time taking in the cider interests of another established Somerset cider-making firm, Whiteways of Whimple. The new company, Coates Gaymers is now part of Allied Breweries.

Gaymer's Olde English: Described as 'the original strong cider, medium dry and full flavoured', this is one of the brand leaders in the cider market. Available as keg or in bottles.

Gaymer's Norfolk Dry: A very dry cider. Available in flagons and bottles.

Coates Somerset Cider: A medium-sweet sparkling cider known to millions by the slogan 'Coates comes up from Somerset, where the cider apples grow.' Available in flagons and bottles.

Coates Farmhouse Special: A strong still cider sold in 2-litre bottles.

Coates Festival Vat: Strong and medium dry. Available in flagons or 2 litre bottles.

Coates Triple Vintage (TV): Strong, still and full-bodied, this is a sweet, richly coloured cider. Available in litre bottles and 2-gallon jars.

Gaymer's Lite: A low-carbohydrate bottled cider introduced in 1979.

Gaymer's Pometta: A sparkling champagne-style cider, available sweet or dry, bottled.

At present Coates Gaymers seem to have little interest in promoting traditional draught cider.

COUNTRYMAN CIDER (NACM)
Felldownhead, Milton Abbot, Tavistock, Devon
Milton Abbot (082 287) 226

Established as a farm cider business for three generations, Felldownhead was bought by Nigel Lawrence and David Atkin in 1978. Under the guidance of Horace Lancaster, the original owner, they are producing cider by traditional methods, with nothing added, nothing taken away.

Their cider is available through some 500 off-licences nationally and 15–20 pubs in Devon and Cornwall.

Their cider museum and off-licence are open Monday–Friday 9–5, all year round; parties by arrangement.

Scrumpy: A full-strength still cider sold on draught or as flagons. Available medium dry or medium sweet.

Gold Label: Still vintage draught cider matured in oak casks for at least three years. Slightly sweeter than scrumpy.

Devon Gold: Medium dry or sweet sparkling bottled cider.

WILLIAM GAYMER & SONS LTD
Station Road, Attleborough, Norfolk
(See *COATES GAYMERS LTD*)

MERRYDOWN WINE plc (NACM)
Horam Manor, Horam, Heathfield, East Sussex
Horam Road (043 53) 2254

When Jack Ward and Ian Howie were demobbed after the last war, they decided to renew an old hobby, and started to make cider in the garage of Jack's cottage called 'Merrydown' in Sussex. They had a hunch that they could make a superior, wine-like cider from the dessert and cooking apples that grew all around them. Their hunch paid off and in 1946 they produced 400 gallons of their Vintage Cider. Nowadays, Merrydown produce around 18,000 bottles a day of their two main ciders.

Widely available in off-licences, supermarkets and some pubs throughout the country. Merrydown don't produce any draught cider.

Vintage Cider: A refreshing, slightly sparkling cider high in alcohol (7½%–8% by volume). Available in bottles of various sizes.

Vintage Dry Cider: Similar in strength and character to Vintage Cider, but drier. Also available in bottles of various sizes.

Strong Still Cider: A medium dry still cider, slightly less strong than the Vintage Ciders. Available as bag-in-box.

Merrydown are also well-known for their apple juice, cider vinegar, mead and country wines.

🍎 R.J. SHEPPY & SON (NACM)
Three Bridges, Bradford-on-Tone, near Taunton, Somerset
Bradford-on-Tone (082 346) 233

The Sheppy family began producing cider commercially in 1925 and have won over 200 awards, including the Gold Medal at the Brewers & Allied Traders Exhibitions in 1932 and 1938.

Available mainly from the Sheppy farm shop, but also stocked by a handful of local pubs and other outlets.

Visitors are welcome to visit the farm, cider museum and farm shop. Cider tasting £1.50 per head. Open Easter – Christmas, 8.30a.m.–dusk, Sundays 12noon–2p.m. (Cider sales only Jan – Easter, Mon–Sat, 8.30a.m.–6p.m.)

Farmhouse Draught Cider: Good quality draught cider. Available dry, medium or sweet.
🍎 *Gold Medal Farmhouse Cider:* A high quality still bottled cider. Available dry, medium or sweet.

SYMONDS' CIDER & ENGLISH WINE COMPANY (NACM)
Stoke Lacy, Bromyard, Hereford & Worcester
Munderfield (088 53) 211

William Symonds M.D. began making cider in 1727, using apples from his orchards at Bodenham in Herefordshire. Since then the family tradition has continued unbroken, although the premises were moved to Stoke Lacy in 1939. Bill Symonds and his son Neville are currently in charge of the business.

The cider is available from Symonds's shop at Stoke Lacy, and through a number of local stockists.

THE CIDER-MAKERS

You can sample the range of Symonds's ciders and perries at the shop before buying. Open Monday–Friday, 9a.m.–7.30p.m.; Saturday and Sunday, 9a.m.–5p.m. (Closed for lunch 1p.m.–2p.m. daily.) Tours of the cider mills can also be arranged (minimum 20 people).

🍎 🍏 *Scrumpy Jack:* An old-fashioned strong cider, fermented naturally with its own yeast.
Luncheon Dry: Dry cider.
Strong Vat: Medium dry cider.
Harvest Vat: Medium sweet cider.
Delicious Sweet: Sweet cider.
🍏 *Old Original Haymaker:* A thirst quenching cider in the old style.
Princess Pippin: Sparkling vintage cider.
🍏 *Barland Dry:* Dry perry.
🍏 *Old Mill:* Medium perry.
🍏 *Moorcroft Sweet:* Sweet perry.

Symonds's ciders and perries are sold in a range of containers and sizes, from half pint and litre bottles to flagons and 5-gallon 'poly kegs'.

They also produce a non-alcoholic cider shandy and a range of English fruit wines.

TAUNTON CIDER COMPANY LTD (NACM)
Norton Fitzwarren, Taunton, Somerset
Taunton (0823) 83141

The story of Taunton cider begins with the Rev. Thomas Cornish, who began making cider at his rectory at Heathfield, near Taunton, back in the 19th century. He even earned the seal of approval from Queen Victoria, and subsequently set up a mill at Norton Fitzwarren with his gardener, Arthur Moor, and a friend, George Pallet. In 1921 the Taunton Cider Company was registered, and its six employees managed to produce 10,000 gallons of cider.

Today Taunton Cider Company is one of the three main cider-makers in the country, and its range of ciders is sold in thousands of outlets throughout the land.

Traditional Draught: Draught cider, available dry or sweet. Only sold in the West Country.

Dry Blackthorn: One of the best known keg dry ciders. Also sold in bottles and cans.

Autumn Gold: High quality, medium sweet keg cider. Also available in bottles and cans.

Special Vat: A strong, medium dry cider, of which Taunton is particularly proud. Available in bottles, cans and bag-in-box.

Exhibition: A strong, still cider, available sweet or dry, and sold in distinctive two-litre glass pitchers.

Pommia: Sparkling champagne-style bottled cider, available medium sweet or dry.

H. WESTON & SONS LTD (NACM)
Much Marcle, Ledbury, Hereford & Worcester
Much Marcle (053 184) 233/4

In 1878, Henry Weston came to farm at The Bounds, Much Marcle, and as a matter of course set about making cider and perry in a small way. Two years later he decided to turn his part-time hobby into a commercial enterprise, and the firm has been going strong ever since.

Weston's now have around 2,500 customers throughout the country and supply draught cider to some 100 pubs mainly in the West Country, London and the Midlands.

Bounds Brand Draught Cider: Described as a very serviceable, everyday draught cider.

🍎 *Farmhouse Rough Cider:* A robust dry cider, normally sold in flagons.

Traditional Country Cider: A dark, medium dry cider, sold in flagons and bottles.

Top Line: A light, sweet, refreshing bottled cider.

Vat 53: A medium dry cider with some of the characteristics of draught cider. Sold in flagons.

🍎 *Supreme Cider:* An extra strong dry cider. Sold in flagons and bottles.

Extra Dry Cider: A thirst-quenching dry cider recommended for cooking. Sold in flagons and bottles.

🍎 *Centenary Cider:* A strong, dry bottled cider introduced for Weston's centenary in 1980.

Special Vintage Cider: A rich, smooth, medium sweet bottled cider made from selected apples and matured for at least a year in oak vats.

🍎 *Perry:* Genuine perry sold in bottles and flagons. Also on draught.

WHITEWAYS OF WHIMPLE LTD (NACM)
Whimple, Exeter, Devon   *Whimple (0404) 822332*

Henry Whiteway started making cider commercially in the 1890s, and for many years his company had a good reputation. In 1961 they became part of the Showerings Group, and in 1968 their cider-making interests were taken over by Coates Gaymers. Whiteways now concentrate on cider vinegar, British wines and the like, although some canned cider still appears under their name (see also *COATES GAYMERS*).

Some other notable cider-makers

BIDDENDEN VINEYARDS
Little Whatmans, Biddenden, Ashford, Kent
Biddenden (0580) 291726

Now the pride of the south-east, Biddenden Vineyards are wine-makers and producers of apple juice and a strong distinctive cider made from the culinary and dessert fruit of the region. They also make Monk's Delight, cider blended with honey and spices, which is excellent for mulling. Visitors are always welcome and guided tours can be booked in advance during the summer. Biddenden cider, a strong cider (available medium or dry) made from the culinary and dessert fruit, is sold in about two dozen Kent pubs and a large number of off-licences in both Kent and Sussex. It is sold in bottles and small 'polycasks'.

V. BLAND
West End Lane, Oldbury-on-Severn, Bristol, Avon
Thornbury (0454) 413124 or 417246

Vernon Bland has been making cider since 1971 and sells his wares from a stall on the A38 near Thornbury. You can't purchase from the farm, though. The draught cider comes either dry, medium or vintage and he also sells bottles of vintage and scrumpy.

E. BROMELL
Bromell's Devon Farm Cider, Lower Uppacott, Tedburn St Mary, Exeter, Devon
Tedburn St Mary (06476) 294

Eric Bromell combines the duties of farmer and cider-maker, and supplies a handful of nearby pubs and off-licences with his powerful cider. He produces four variations on the draught theme – dry, medium, medium-sweet and sweet. Visitors can also buy from the farm.

V. CHURCHWARD
Yalberton Farm, Paignton, Devon   *Paignton (0803) 558157*

Vic Churchward's family has been making cider on their farm since 1947, using mixed cider apples which are fermented naturally to produce four kinds of still draught cider: dry, Devon mix, medium and sweet. You can buy from the farm, or sample it in about ten Devon pubs (and one or two in Cornwall).

JOHN DIX
Dixie's Fine Ciders, Marchioness Sheds, Commercial Road, Bathurst Basin, Bristol, Avon
Bristol (0272) 276596

John Dix, known to everyone as Dixie, has been the scourge of the cider-making giants for a number of years, and is still an outspoken champion of true traditional cider. He is also a man of his word and makes his cider without any compromises to modern trends. The place to sample his brews – Apple Cider, Vintage Cider and Cripple Cock (true!) – is the Marchioness Sheds, indeed Dixie's cider isn't sold in any local pubs, although it's marketed by Saffron Ciders, who distribute it to parts of East Anglia.

I. & S. DUNKERTON
Hays Head, Luntley, Pembridge, Leominster,
Hereford & Worcester
Pembridge (05447) 653   *(cont'd over)*

Ivor and Susie Dunkerton make excellent draught cider from a range of genuine cider apples, old and new, including Foxwhelp, Yarlington Mill, Brown Snout, Brown Thorn, Medaille D'or, Michelin, Dabinett, Kingston Black and Cider Ladies Finger. Their aim is to produce cider that has the character of a wine. Also look out for their perry, made in a similar fashion from famous varieties such as Moorcroft, Barland, Blakeney Red and Red Horse. You can buy both from the farm, sample the cider at the Saracen's Head in Hereford or buy it from one of a handful of off-licences.

‌ ‌ R. FLEMING
Auberrow House, Wellington, near Hereford, Hereford & Worcester
Canon Pyon (043 271) 558

Richard Fleming's draught cider is well-respected among connoisseurs of the real thing. It is made from classic cider apples like Foxwhelp and Kingston Black without any additives (apart from a little sugar in the sweeter brands). Available medium sweet, medium, dry and vintage. A small number of pubs stock it and it's also obtainable from the farm.

‌ T. GRAY
Halstow, Tedburn St Mary, Exeter, Devon
Tedburn St Mary (064 76) 236

Generations of the Gray family have been making cider here for the last 300 years and they are currently producing around 20,000 gallons per year from old-fashioned bittersweets. Tom Gray's draught cider, which is available dry, medium or sweet, is sold at the farm and in a handful of Devon pubs.

F. HILL & SON
Barkingdon Manor, Staverton, near Totnes, Devon
Staverton (080 426) 239

Hill's cider has been going strong for almost 50 years and Richard Hill is continuing the tradition, offering a range of sweet, medium and dry draught ciders made from bittersweet apples grown in his own orchards and by local farmers. You can buy the cider from the farm shop and sample it in something like 80 pubs, mostly in south Devon and Cornwall.

S. INCH
Bean Park, Hatherleigh Road, Winkleigh, Devon
Winkleigh (083 783) 363

Sam Inch's draught cider finds its way into a handful of north Devon pubs, and there's a good choice ranging from sweet, medium and dry to the potent Harvest Scrumpy.

H. PERRY
The Cider Mills, Dowlish Wake, Ilminster, Somerset
Ilminster (046 05) 2681

Henry Perry and his wife make cider in an old 16th-century thatched barn, and they also run a shop where you can purchase their wares and lots more besides. Perry's draught cider comes in two brands, Farmhouse and Vintage, both available sweet, medium or dry. It is also sold in a few local pubs.

G. RICH
Mill Farm, Watchfield, Highbridge, Somerset
Burnham-on-Sea (0278) 783651 (cont'd over)

Gordon Rich's cider is available dry or sweet and is sold on the farm, as well as in a number of nearby pubs.

J. TEMPERLEY
Burrow Hill Cider, Pass Vale Farm, Burrow Hill, Kingsbury Episcopi, Martock, Somerset
South Petherton (0460) 40782

Julian Temperley is a great campaigner for real cider, and his excellent brews have won him many prizes. He has over 4,000 trees bearing famous cider apples like Kingston Black, Brown Snout, Chisel Jersey, Yarlington Mill and Somerset Redstreak, and is continuing a tradition of cider-making at Burrow Hill going back over 100 years. Buy from the farm, or sample the cider in one of the nearby pubs that sell it.

J. THATCHER
Myrtle Farm, Sandford, near Bristol, Avon
Banwell (0934) 822862

John Thatcher's thriving firm recently amalgamated with Peter Champeney's Cheddar Valley Cider Company across the road, but both continue to produce cider. Thatcher's is traditional draught, as well as clear still cider and a sparkling cider too. It can be purchased in some local pubs and off-licences, and even finds its way to the Midlands and South Wales.

W.J. VICKERY
Hisbeers Farm, Buckland St Mary, Chard, Somerset
Buckland St Mary (046 034) 378

Take a trip to the Vickerys' farm to purchase some of their excellent draught cider, or track it down in one or two Somerset pubs.

R. WILKINS
Lands End Farm, Mudgley, Wedmore, Somerset
Wedmore (0934) 712385

Roger Wilkins makes splendid cider from apples such as Bulmer's Norman, Yarlington Mill, Somerset Redstreak and Tremletts Bitter. His dry cider has nothing added to it, although the medium and sweet brands do contain some sweetener. Sold on the farm and draught in about twenty Somerset pubs and clubs.

C. WILLIAMS
Meadowsweet Cider, Meadowsweet Farm, Bicknoller, near Taunton, Somerset
Stogumber (098 46) 409

The emphasis here is on natural produce, from goat's cheese to traditional cider, which are sold on the farm. The cider can also be tasted in about half a dozen local pubs selling Clive Williams's authentic brew.

6
CIDER
CUSTOMS

'AULD CIDER'

FOR centuries cider had a place in many of the important seasonal customs and rituals associated with the progress of the year: the spring awakening, planting crops, harvesting, Christmas and the year's turning. In the western counties of England – and in the south as well – where cider was the common drink of the people, it was the natural accompaniment to any gathering or celebration.

Many of these customs centred around the lighting of bonfires on New Year's Eve to protect the wheat crop. One ancient Herefordshire tradition involved setting fire to a bundle of hawthorn twigs that had been hung up in a cottage like mistletoe right through the year. This 'burning bush' was carried out into the field, twelve bundles of hay were lit from it and these were dragged over twelve ridges of the old field system.

Then the men stand in a ring round the fire and 'holloa auld cider'. They sing on one very deep note, very slowly, holding each syllable as long as possible. 'Auld Ci–der'. The 'der' becomes a sort of growl at the end, and is an octave below the first two notes; it has a weird dirge-like effect. This is repeated thrice, bowing as low as possible as each note is sung, nine bows altogether. Then follows cheering and drinking, cider and cake being provided for the purpose.*

* *The Folk-Lore of Herefordshire* by E.M.Leather, 1912

Across the English Channel, in the cider-producing region of Normandy, it was once the custom for bands of men, women and children to invade the orchards on Epiphany Eve, or the first Sunday in Lent, to throw lighted torches against the apple trees and make little bonfires under their branches. The aim was to bless the trees and invoke prosperous growth, even at the risk of scorching the leaves and branches in the process.

TOASTING THE TREES

The most significant and famous ritual in which cider became involved was 'wassailing'. The word 'wassail' comes from the Anglo Saxon *waes hael*, meaning 'be of good health'; in other words it was a toast, the way in which our ancestors said 'cheers' and drank each other's health. Naturally there was great wassailing during the festive Christmas season: the master of the house would gather his family round the wassail bowl which was probably filled with a warming brew called 'lamb's wool' made from ale, spices, sugar and crab apples. Shakespeare described 'rosted crabs hissing in the bowl', and no doubt cider found its place in the bowl too. There would be singing and dancing as the bowl was passed round and people toasted each other.

But wassailing wasn't confined to humans. It was until quite recently the custom to wassail the apple orchards on Twelfth Night. In the apple-growing areas of south-west England this ceremony was carried out among the trees themselves; it was acted out to protect them from evil spirits, to wake them up and give them life so that they produced a heavy crop the following year.

In the heyday of this custom, when people believed instinctively in the powerful pagan symbolism at the heart of the ritual, it was an amazing scene. A gang of farmworkers would head for the orchard, singing and shouting as they went; they would pick out the biggest tree to represent the whole orchard, stand round it and await the arrival of a big steaming pan of cider. They poured some cider on its roots, dipped its lowest branches in the hot brew and put pieces of cider-soaked toast among its leaves as an offering to Pomona, the goddess of fruits. Then the men drank, each in turn, and wassailed the tree as if it were a friend. The toasts varied, but this was a great favourite:

> *Here's to thee, old apple tree,*
> *Whence thou may'st bud and whence thou may'st blow*
> *And when thou may'st bear apples enow.*
> *Hats full, caps full, bushel, bushel sacks full,*
> *And my pockets full too!*
> *Hurrah!*

The men quaffed more cider, then made as much noise as possible, blasting shotguns into the trees, banging on buckets, yelling and ringing bells. Anything to scare off the evil spirits of winter and wake up the trees.

Timid, half-hearted revivals of wassailing still take place, especially in a handful of West Country pubs, but the ritual has none of its old power. It's either an excuse for drinking, dancing and a boozy frolic, or it's used as a publicity stunt to encourage people to drink more of a particular brand of cider.

7

WHERE TO FIND
GOOD CIDER

In this chapter I have put together a personal selection of my favourite pubs, cider houses, cider bars and other places where drinkers can enjoy traditional cider. I have also added a few of the best off-licences and centres where cider can be bought to take away.

The ciders listed are, for the most part, available on draught, although one or two, e.g. Aspall and Merrydown, are only served from the bottle. Keg ciders are not included at all.

Traditional draught cider is now available in most English counties, even in the far north, but there are still one or two deserts, for instance Cheshire and Humberside. Hopefully it will not be long before even these regions have their share of cider pubs and off-licences.

NOTE: While every effort has been made to ensure the accuracy of each entry, circumstances can alter – pubs may change hands or close, landlords may give up selling cider, or try a different brand, for instance. Therefore neither the author nor the publishers can accept any liability for information which may subsequently be found to be incorrect.

Listings are compiled by county: beginning with London, then alphabetically through the rest of England and Wales.

ENGLAND

London

Chimes English Cider & Wine Bar
26, Churton Street, Pimlico, SW1 *01-821 7456*
An airy, attractive and thoroughly appealing cider/wine bar. Serious drinking and snacks upstairs; restaurant food in the basement (excellent pies). *Aspall cyder, Merrydown cider, Weston's cider & perry*

Chiswell Vaults
Chiswell Street, EC1 *01-588 5733*
A rambling basement cellar bar, in the vaults of Whitbread's old cellars. Good food and good drink attracts a big crowd at lunchtimes. *Bulmer's cider*

Cranks
8, Marshall Street, W1 *01-437 9431*
Peter Robinson's, Oxford Circus, W1 *01-580 6214*
11, The Market, Covent Garden, WC2 *01-379 6508*
The wholefood specialists, offering healthy, organically produced cider. Delicious vegetarian food served. *Aspall cyder*

Dickens Inn
St Katherine's Way, St Katherine's Dock, E1 *01-488 2208*
Imaginatively built from an 18th-century dockside warehouse to create the style of a Georgian inn. Bar snacks and full meals. *Bulmer's cider*

George
77, Borough High Street, Southwark, SE1 *01-407 2056*
London's only surviving galleried inn, rebuilt in 1676. Snacks, salads and full meals. *Bulmer's cider*

Grafton
2, Strutton Ground, Victoria, SW1 *01-799 1029*
A busy, dark pub alongside Strutton Ground market. Bare boards and sawdust on the floor. Bar food. *Bulmer's cider*

Great British Beer Factory
148, Old Brompton Road, SW5
Beer is the name of the game here, and most of the pints are sold at a discount. *Bulmer's cider*

Museum Tavern
49, Great Russell Street, WC1 *01-242 8987*
A smart, Victorian-style pub opposite the British Museum. Bar food. *Bulmer's cider*

Page & Henry (off-licence only)
Crown Road, St Margarets, Twickenham. *Dunkerton's cider*

Sherlock Holmes
10, Northumberland Street, WC2 *01-930 2644*
Devotees of the great detective will relish the collection of
Holmes bric-à-brac on show at this popular pub. Lunchtime bar
food. *Bulmer's cider*

Avon

BRISTOL
The Brewery Stores (off-licence only)
125, Two Mile Hill Road, Kingswood *Bristol (0272) 672154.*
Thatcher's cider, Weston's cider & perry

BRISTOL
Coronation Tap
Sion Place, Clifton *Bristol (0272) 739617*
A crowded traditional pub, popular with city drinkers. Look for
the rows of big cider barrels. *Bulmer's cider, Taunton cider*

OLDBURY-ON-SEVERN
Anchor Inn
Thornbury (0454) 413331
A remote village pub boasting an excellent range of beers and fine
food, ranging from rabbit pie to traditional Oldbury tart packed
with gooseberries. Garden. *Bulmer's cider*

OLD SODBURY
Dog Inn
Badminton Road *Chipping Sodbury (0454) 312006*

Imaginative seafood dishes and robust meaty fare draw the crowds to this 18th-century roadside inn. Garden. *Bulmer's cider*

SOUTHSTOKE
Pack Horse
No fewer than three shove-halfpenny tables make this 15th-century village pub a popular venue for fans of pub games. *Coates cider*

Bedfordshire

DEEPDALE
Locomotive
Potton (0767) 260365
Close to the RSPB headquarters, this pleasant country pub is popular with thirsty ornithologists. Occasional barn dances and barbecues. Garden. *Bulmer's cider*

TEMPSFORD
Anchor
Biggleswade (0767) 40233
A large pub just off the A1, with a huge garden by the banks of the River Ouse. Snacks and restaurant meals. *Bulmer's cider*

TURVEY
Three Fyshes
Turvey (023 064) 264
An old-fashioned but stylish pub on the A428, Bedford-Northampton Road. Attractions include well kept beers, table skittles and simple, nourishing food. Garden. *Bland's cider*

Berkshire

FIFIELD
Royal Foresters Cider House
Drift Road *Maidenhead (0628) 27987*
Set up by Bulmer's as a showcase for all their ciders. Also sells
Calvados. *Bulmer's cider*

HURLEY
Black Boy
Henley Road *Littlewick Green (062 882) 4212*
Dating back to the 16th century, this old beamed tavern is now a
comfortable roadside pub. Food, Garden. *Merrydown cider*

KINTBURY
Crossways Inn
Inkpen Road *Kintbury (0488) 58398*
Formerly a school, this pleasant gabled pub is surrounded by the
lovely countryside of the Kennet Valley. Snacks and meals.
Garden. *Bulmer's cider*

Buckinghamshire

AKELEY
Bull & Butcher
The Square *Lillingstone Dayrell (028 06) 257*
A cosy village pub on the A413. The country-made bread is
highly praised. Garden. *Weston's cider*

HAMBLEDEN
Stag & Huntsman
Hambleden (049 166) 227

Home-brewed beer vies with cider as the attraction in this village pub. Useful bed and breakfast too. Garden. *Bulmer's cider*

MARSH GIBBON
Greyhound Inn
Stratton Audley (086 97) 365
A splendid 16th-century pub with its own brewery. Excellent food in the beamed bar at lunchtime. Garden. Closed Monday lunchtime. *Weston's cider*

MARSWORTH
Red Lion
Vicarage Road *Cheddington (0296) 668366*
Close to the Grand Union Canal and Tring Reservoirs Nature Reserve, this is a very busy weekend and summer pub. It's also a regular stop for local morris dancers. Wholesome food. *Weston's cider*

RAVENSTONE
Wheatsheaf
Stoke Goldington (090 855) 278
The beer is served from an old bakery oven at this village pub. Garden. *Bland's cider*

Cambridgeshire

CAMBRIDGE
Bath-Cambridge Cider House
Benet Street
Right in the centre of the city, this beamed cider house is a popular local watering place. Hot and cold food. *Bulmer's cider*

CAMBRIDGE
Salisbury Arms
Tenison Road *Cambridge (0223) 60363*
This pub needs to be big, for it's always packed with throngs of drinkers sampling the impressive range of traditional beers as well as the cider. Lunchtime food. *Weston's cider*

KIRTLING
Queens Head
Newmarket (0638) 730253
A fine Elizabethan pub noted for its food (anything from smoked haddock soup to savoury pies). Good bed and breakfast. Garden. *Bulmer's cider*

PETERBOROUGH
Martins Wine Shop (off-licence only)
143, Oundle Road, Woodston *Peterborough (0733) 310926*
Symonds' cider & perry

STILTON
Bell Inn
High Street *Peterborough (0733) 242626*
Stilton cheese was first served here back in the 18th century. After years lying derelict, this historic inn has been brought back to life in grand style. The Stilton is a must. *Weston's cider*

Cleveland

STOCKTON-ON-TEES
Cricketers Arms
Portrack Lane *Stockton-on-Tees (0642) 65468*

One of Bulmer's most northerly outposts. A typical revamped town pub. *Bulmer's cider*

Cornwall

ALBASTON
Queens Head
near Gunnislake *Tavistock (0822) 832482*
A popular local pub in an old mining area. *Countryman cider, Taunton cider*

CHILSWORTHY
White Hart Inn
Tavistock (0822) 832307
There are lovely views of the Tamar Valley from this pub. Look out for the guest beers as well as the cider. Garden. *Countryman cider, Taunton cider*

MANACCAN
New Inn
Manaccan (032 623) 323
A lovely old thatched pub kept in very good order. Food available might include frankfurters with bubble and squeak or Chinese liver casserole. Garden. *Merrydown cider*

MENHENIOT
White Hart
Liskeard (0579) 42245
Open log fires and beams create a warm, friendly atmosphere in this peacefully situated 17th-century pub. Snacks and full meals. *Merrydown cider*

POLGOOTH
Polgooth Inn
St Austell (0726) 4089
A converted farmhouse with plenty of animals still in residence.
Very much a local. Snacks and full meals. Garden. *Merrydown cider*

POLKERRIS
Rashleigh Inn
Par (072 681) 3991
Superbly positioned beneath the cliffs and with a terrace by the
beach, this pub can be packed out during the summer. The
lunchtime cold buffet is particularly popular. Garden. *Bulmer's cider*

Cumbria

ELTERWATER
Britannia Inn
Langdale (096 67) 210
Thirsty hikers can call in at this 400-year-old stone inn for
refreshment. Useful bed and breakfast. Garden. *Bulmer's cider*

LOWESWATER
Kirkstile Inn
Near Cockermouth *Lorton (090 085) 219*
Glorious scenery is one of the main attractions at this cosy 16th-
century inn up in the fells. Garden. *Bulmer's cider*

Derbyshire

DRONFIELD
Old Sidings
91, Chesterfield Road
Railway buffs will appreciate the decor and theme of this aptly
named pub. *Bulmer's cider*

MAREHAY
Hollybush
Brook Lane *Ripley (0773) 42558*
In summer you can watch the local team play cricket from this
tastefully modernized pub. Garden. *Bulmer's cider*

Devon

ASHPRINGTON
Waterman's Arms
Bow Bridge *Harbertonford (080 423) 214*
A comfortable oak-beamed pub by the little River Harbourne.
Mammoth salads are favourites on the menu. Garden. *Hill's
cider*

ASHBURTON
Exeter Inn
26, West Street *Ashburton (0364) 52559*
A splendid little pub, said to date back to the 12th century.
Highly recommended bed and breakfast. Garden. *Hill's cider*

BANTHAM
Sloop Inn
Near Thurlestone *Thurlestone (054 857) 489*   (cont'd over)

Old sea-dogs still frequent this 16th-century inn, which has nautical decor and was once a smugglers' haunt. Simple snacks, useful bed and breakfast. *Hill's cider*

BROADHEMBURY
Drewe Arms
Broadhembury (040 484) 267
There's still plenty of history in this delightful 15th-century thatched inn with its beams, panelling and mullioned windows with old soda-glass panes. Good value bar snacks. Garden. *Bulmer's cider*

BURGH ISLAND
Pilchard Inn
Near Bigbury-on-Sea *Bigbury-on-Sea (054 881) 344*
Three hundred yards across the sands from Bigbury. Go on foot at low tide, or use the special tractor. An extraordinary old pub perched above the sands. Snacks and bar meals in season. *Taunton cider*

DARTINGTON
Cott Inn
Totnes (0803) 863777
Built in 1320 for local mine-owner John Cott, this old thatched inn still has a feel of the past about it. Superb cold buffet plus hot dishes. Homely accommodation. Garden. *Hill's cider*

DARTINGTON
Dartington Farm Food Shop (off-licence only)
Cider Press Centre, Shinners Bridge *Totnes (0803) 864171*
Specializes in the best that Devon has to offer in the way of food and drink. *Hill's cider*

FROGMORE
Globe Inn
Near Kingsbridge *Frogmore (054 853) 351*
A pleasant pub with a distinctly nautical theme: note the paintings of ships that have circumnavigated the globe. Useful bed and breakfast. *Hill's cider*

HARBERTON
Church House Inn
Totnes (0803) 863707
A peaceful village pub that can trace its history back to Norman times, and still boasts some fine oak panelling and a fragile latticed glass window. Simple snacks. *Churchward's cider*

HEXWORTHY
Forest Inn
Poundsgate (036 43) 211
Salmon fishing and pony trekking are popular attractions at this friendly Dartmoor pub. Bed and breakfast. *Hill's cider*

HORNDON
Elephant's Nest Inn
Near Mary Tavy *Mary Tavy (082 281) 273*
A 400-year-old white-painted inn with fine views across the moors. Good beers and nourishing bar food. Garden. *Countryman cider*

HORN'S CROSS
Hoops Inn
Near Bideford *Horn's Cross (023 75) 222*
A lovely old 13th-century thatched pub. Excellent accommodation. *Bulmer's cider*

LUTTON
Mountain Inn
Plymouth (0752) 837247
Beams, a log fire and a grandfather clock set the tone in this
old-fashioned village pub. Wholesome lunchtime snacks (try the
home-made pasties). Terrace outside. *Countryman cider*

LYMPSTONE
Globe Inn
Exmouth (0395) 263166
Fresh seafood is irresistible in this popular pub in the heart of a
fishing village. *Coates Gaymer's cider*

PETER TAVY
Peter Tavy Inn
Near Tavistock *Mary Tavy (082 281) 348*
Superb local beers and some outstanding food are the great
features of this tiny 14th-century pub. Barbecues at the weekend
(weather permitting). There are picnic tables under the fruit
trees in the garden. *Bulmer's cider*

RINGMORE
Journey's End Inn
Bigbury-on-Sea (054 881) 205
R.C.Sherriff wrote his great anti-war play here, and the pub was
re-named after it. An ancient hostelry dating back 600 years.
Good bed and breakfast. Garden. *Bulmer's cider*

SOUTH ZEAL
Oxenham Arms
Sticklepath (083 784) 244
An elegant Tudor mansion with its fair share of traditional

features. Bar snacks and accommodation. Stone monastery steps
lead up to the garden. *Gray's cider*

STICKLEPATH
Devonshire
Sticklepath (083 784) 626
An old thatched pub just off the main A30. Pay a visit to the
working waterpower and crafts museum in the village. *Gray's
cider*

Dorset

ANSTY
Fox Inn
Near Dorchester *Milton Abbas (0258) 880328*
A busy brick and flint pub renowned for its spectacular cold
buffet. Home-brewed beer too. *Taunton cider*

EVERSHOT
Acorn
Fore Street *Evershot (093 583) 228*
Mentioned in Hardy's *Tess of the D'Urbervilles*, when it was
called the Sow and Acorn. Plenty of food and pleasant accom-
modation. A skittle alley draws the crowds. *Taunton cider*

SHAVE CROSS
Shave Cross Inn
Marshwood Vale *Broadwindsor (0308) 68358*
Medieval monks used to stop at this fine old inn to have their
tonsures shaved (hence the name). Simple lunchtime snacks.
Garden. Closed Mondays, except Bank Holidays. *Taunton cider
(summer only)*

Essex

BRIGHTLINGSEA
Barwell & Jones (off-licence only)
21, High Street *Brightlingsea (020 630) 2115*
Aspall cyder

DEDHAM
Lamb
Lamb Corner
A fine old 15th-century hostelry in the heart of Constable
country. Garden. *Bulmer's cider*

EPPING
Forest Gate
Bell Common
As its name suggests, this old pub is right on the fringes of
Epping Forest. Garden. *Bulmer's cider*

TIPTREE
Barwell & Jones (off-licence only)
16, Maldon Road *Tiptree (0621) 815453*
Aspall cyder

Gloucestershire

BROADWELL
Fox Inn
Stow-on-the-Wold (0451) 30212
Traditional pub games, nourishing food and cosy accommoda-
tion are features of this little village pub. Garden. *Weston's cider*

BROCKWEIR
Brockweir Inn
Tintern (029 18) 548
There are nice views of the Wye Valley and Tintern Abbey from the pathways around this sturdily furnished pub. Food and simple accommodation. Garden. *Bulmer's cider*

GLASSHOUSE
Glasshouse Inn
May Hill, Longhope *Gloucester (0452) 830529*
A relatively untouched pub at the foot of May Hill. Garden. *Bulmer's cider, Symonds' cider*

LECHLADE
Crown Inn
High Street *Faringdom (0367) 52218*
A simple Cotswold village pub famed for its food – meaty hamburgers are particularly popular. Walled garden. *Weston's cider*

LITTLE WASHBOURNE
Hobnails Inn
Near Tewkesbury *Alderton (024 262) 237*
This popular little pub has been in the same family for two centuries. Excellent baps to go with your tipple. *Bulmer's cider*

NORTH NIBLEY
New Inn
Dursley (0453) 3659
A lovely pub hidden away in the Gloucestershire countryside. Excellent draught beers (also a display of antique beer engines). Delightful garden with swings under the fruit trees. *Inch's cider*

SAPPERTON
Daneway Inn
Daneway *Frampton Mansell (028 576) 297*
Set in a wooded valley by the River Frome and the derelict
Thames and Severn Canal. Attractive garden. *Bulmer's cider*

WINCHCOMBE
Old Corner Cupboard Inn
Gloucester Street *Winchcombe (0242) 602303*
An attractive old sandstone pub. Good hearty snacks and meals
at lunchtime. Little garden. *Bulmer's cider*

Hampshire

FROYLE
Hen & Chicken
Lower Froyle *Bentley (0420) 72115*
Parts of this old pub date back to Tudor times and it still has a
feeling of history. Bar snacks and full meals. Garden. *Bulmer's
cider*

SOUTHAMPTON
Canute Cider House
Canute Road *Southampton (0703) 24188*
A new cider house owned by Whitbread brewery. *Bulmer's cider*

STOCKBRIDGE
White Hart
High Street *Andover (0264) 810475*
A comfortable pub combining the best of old and new. Good
choice of delicious food, excellent beers and useful accommoda-
tion. *Taunton cider*

Hereford & Worcester

CANON PYON
Nag's Head
Canon Pyon (043 271) 252
A delightful village pub with food and garden. *Fleming's cider*

CAREY
Cottage of Content
Carey (043 270) 242
Refreshment was first served here in 1485, when one of the cottagers opened an ale and cider parlour; it has been going strong ever since. Bar snacks, restaurant meals and homely accommodation. There's a cider press in the garden. *Bulmer's cider*

DEFFORD
Monkey House
Evesham (0386) 750234
Probably the most legendary of all cider houses. A unique, rough-and-ready place for which Bulmer's produce a special brew. *Bulmer's cider*

HEREFORD
Saracen's Head
St Martin's Street *Hereford (0432) 57480*
A popular pub just by the old Wye Bridge. Cold table and snacks at lunchtime. Garden. *Dunkerton's cider, Bulmer's cider*

HEREFORD
The Shop under the Clock (off-licence only)
11, Commercial Road *Hereford (0432) 268279* (cont'd over)

Bulmer's cider, Dunkerton's cider and perry, Fleming's cider, Symonds' cider and perry, Weston's cider and perry, and others.

LEDBURY
Feathers Hotel
High Street *Ledbury (0531) 2600*
A splendid Elizabethan half-timbered hostelry. Smart and stylish within. Excellent accommodation. *Weston's cider*

WHITNEY-ON-WYE
Rhydspence Inn
Clifford (049 73) 262
A gem of a 14th-century inn, renowned for its friendliness, hospitality, good beer and cider, superb food and comfortable accommodation. Closed all Monday & Tuesday lunchtime in winter, also 2 weeks November. *Fleming's cider*

Hertfordshire

ALDBURY
Valiant Trooper
Trooper Road *Aldbury Common (044 285) 203*
A lively, revitalized pub in a much-photographed village. Simple lunchtime snacks. Garden. *Bulmer's cider*

ALDENHAM
Church Farm Shop (off-licence only)
Radlett (092 76) 7443
Weston's cider

COLNEY HEATH
Crooked Billet
88, High Street *Bowmansgreen (0727) 22128*

The local blacksmith built this pub as a cottage alehouse back in the 18th century. Good range of beers. Garden. *Bulmer's cider*

OLD BRICKET WOOD
Old Fox
School Lane *Garston (092 73) 73083*
Tucked away at the end of a long wooded lane, this pub has retained its feeling of cosy isolation. Garden. *Coates Gaymers cider*

Kent

BIDDENDEN
Three Chimneys
Biddenden (0580) 291472
Situated a mile out of the village on the road to Sissinghurst. An archetypal country pub boasting local cider, a good range of beers and excellent food (from smoked haddock in cheese sauce to game pie). Lovely garden too. *Biddenden cider*

CHIDDINGSTONE
Castle Inn
Penshurst (0892) 870247
A fine old pub in a National Trust village. Bar snacks and restaurant meals. Garden. *Bulmer's cider*

GROOMBRIDGE
Crown Inn
Near Tunbridge Wells *Groombridge (089 276) 361*
A fine old 16th-century pub, full of beams and cosy nooks and crannies. Useful bed and breakfast. Garden. *Biddenden cider*

ICKHAM
Duke William
The Street *Littlebourne (022 778) 308*
An attractive pub in the centre of the village. Interesting food
from salt beef to oyster pudding. Attractive garden. *Biddenden
cider*

SMARDEN
Bell
Bell Lane *Smarden (023 377) 283*
A classic weatherboarded Kentish pub noted for its good range of
beers, local cider and appetizing food. Comfortable accommoda-
tion, too. *Biddenden cider*

SPELDHURST
George & Dragon
Langton (089 286) 3125
One of the oldest hostelries in the south-east (it's said that
Kentish archers slept here after the Battle of Agincourt in 1415).
Good choice of bar food and restaurant meals. Little garden.
Bulmer's cider

Lancashire

CLEVELEYS
Tap House (off-licence only)
32, Cumberland Avenue *Cleveleys (0253) 854578*
Symonds' cider

SLAIDBURN
Hark to Bounty Inn
Near Clitheroe *Slaidburn (020 06) 246*

A 13th-century village pub in the Forest of Bowland, noted for its friendliness and hospitality. Snacks and full meals; good accommodation. Garden. *Merrydown cider*

SNATCHEMS
Golden Ball
Lancaster Road
If the tide is very high you may be cut off inside this pub on the banks of the River Lune. Garden. *Bulmer's cider*

Leicestershire

HINCKLEY
Black Horse
Upper Bond Street *Hinckley (0455) 637613*
Situated in the centre of town, this is a popular and cosy local haunt. *Bulmer's cider*

KINGS MILLS
Priest House Hotel
Castle Donington *Derby (0332) 810649*
Part of a historic site on the banks of the River Trent, mentioned in the Domesday Book. Excellent accommodation and nourishing food. *Bulmer's cider*

Lincolnshire

ASWARBY
Tally Ho
Near Sleaford *Culverthorpe (052 95) 205*
A rustic 17th-century stone inn with hunting and farming associations. Modern annexe accommodation. Garden. *Bulmer's cider*

83

LINCOLN
Small Beer (off-licence only)
91, Newland Street *Lincoln (0522) 28628*
Symonds' cider

STAMFORD
Scotgate Inn
Scotgate *Stamford (0780) 52901*
The flagship of Melbourns's brewery, with a museum next door.
Hot and cold food. *Bulmer's cider*

Norfolk

HARLESTON
Barwell & Jones (off-licence only)
The Thoroughfare *Harleston (0379) 852243*
Aspall cyder

NORWICH
Barwell & Jones (off-licence only)
8, Dixons Fold *Norwich (0603) 49043*
Aspall cyder

NORWICH
Horse & Dray
137, Ber Street *Norwich (0603) 24741*
A comfortable and popular city pub. Bar food. Outdoor drinking. *Bulmer's cider*

Northamptonshire

NORTHAMPTON
King William IV
Commercial Street *Northampton (0604) 21307*
Right in the middle of town, this is a very busy and popular pub.
Large selection of traditional beers. Food at lunchtime. *Weston's
cider*

NORTHAMPTON
Northampton Beer Agency (off-licence only)
34, Derby Road *Northampton (0604) 37670*
Bland's cider

WEEDON
Narrowboat
Stowe Hill *Weedon (0327) 40354*
An aptly named pub with a garden sloping down to the banks of
the Grand Union canal. Good choice of meals and snacks.
Bulmer's cider

WESTON
Crown
Sulgrave (029 576) 382
A friendly, flagstoned pub in an attractive village (no prizes for
guessing which cider they serve!). Bar food. Garden. *Weston's
cider*

Nottinghamshire

MAPLEBECK
Beehive

(cont'd over)

A tiny little pub surrounded by open countryside. A peaceful, cosy atmosphere prevails. Bar snacks. Garden. *Bulmer's cider*

NOTTINGHAM
Real Thing Off-Licence (off-licence only)
186–188, Mansfield Road *Nottingham (0602) 599368*
Inch's cider, Perry's cider, Symonds' cider, Weston's cider, and others.

Oxfordshire

BURFORD
Lamb Inn
Sheep Street *Burford (099 382) 3155*
A delightful Cotswold-stone inn, oozing charm and character. Restaurant and lunchtime bar snacks. Old-fashioned accommodation. Lovely cottage garden. *Bulmer's cider*

HOOK NORTON
Gate Hangs High
Sibford Road *Hook Norton (0608) 737387*
Once a toll-house with the motto: 'This gate hangs high and hinders none, refresh and pay, and travel on.' Today's travellers still appreciate the refreshment (liquid and solid) on offer. Garden. *Bulmer's cider*

OXFORD
Bear
Alfred Street *Oxford (0865) 44680*
A genuinely old-fashioned pub tucked away down a narrow street in the city centre. Bedecked with thousands of club ties. Simple food. *Coates Gaymers cider*

OXFORD
Turf Tavern
5, Bath Place, Holywell Street *Oxford (0865) 243235*
This 'low-ceilinged tavern up a court' described by Hardy in
Jude the Obscure is now an Oxford institution. Tasty hot and
cold food; cosy accommodation. Courtyard garden. *Weston's
cider*

SOUTH LEIGH
Mason Arms
Near Witney *Witney (0993) 2485*
A lovely thatched pub noted for its delicious food and excellent
home-brewed Sowlye Ale, which makes a worthy alternative to
cider. Garden. Closed Mondays. *Bulmer's cider*

Shropshire

BISHOP'S CASTLE
Three Tuns
Salop Street *Bishop's Castle (0588) 638797*
The beer's the thing at this ancient home-brew pub, first men-
tioned in 1642. Cider and simple food. Garden. *Weston's cider*

LLANFAIR WATERDINE
Red Lion
Knighton (0547) 528214
A friendly stone-built inn on the banks of the River Teme. The
food is simple and tasty; the accommodation cosy. Garden.
Bulmer's cider

WOOTON
Cider House

(cont'd over)

A genuine cider house, selling nothing else (except hot and cold bar snacks). Garden. *Bulmer's cider*

Somerset

BRENDON HILLS
Ralegh's Cross Inn
Near Watchet *Washford (0984) 40343*
Isolated at a crossroads among the wilds of Exmoor. Accommodation (some in the bungalow annexe). Garden. *Meadowsweet cider* (made by C. Williams)

CASTLE CARY
White Hart
Fore Street *Castle Cary (0963) 50255*
A convivial 17th-century coaching inn, beautifully renovated. Snacks and full meals; accommodation. *Taunton cider*

GLASTONBURY
Rifleman's Arms
Chilkwell Street *Glastonbury (0458) 31023*
Just a little walk from Glastonbury Tor, this low-ceilinged ancient pub is a haven for lovers of beer and cider. *Taunton cider, Wilkins cider*

LANGLEY MARSH
Three Horseshoes
Wiveliscombe (0984) 23763
Splendid and unusual bar food (try the traditional stargazey pasty) is a major attraction at this delightful village pub. Good beers and cider to match. Garden. *Perry's cider*

MILBORNE PORT
Queen's Head
Milborne Port (0963) 250314
Beams and bare stone walls create a rustic atmosphere in this
former coaching inn. Varied choice of beers. Snacks at lunch-
time. Courtyard. *Taunton cider*

PORLOCK
Ship
Porlock (0643) 862507
Nestling beneath steep Porlock Hill, this charming old thatched
cottage is a friendly place to visit. Bar snacks and restaurant
meals. Garden. *Perry's cider*

STAPLE FITZPAINE
Greyhound Inn
Hatch Beauchamp (0823) 480227
A tranquil setting, a friendly welcome, fine food and excellent
liquid refreshment continue to make this village pub an excep-
tional hostelry. Accommodation too. *Taunton cider*

STOGUMBER
White Horse Inn
Stogumber (098 46) 277
A large roomy pub off the A358. Bar snacks and restaurant
meals. Garden. *Meadowsweet cider* (made by C. Williams),
Sheppy's cider

Staffordshire

BURSLEM
Travellers Rest
239, Newcastle Street *Stoke-on-Trent (0782) 810418*

(cont'd over)

This modern roadside pub offers a wide choice of food at lunchtime, from cold joints to rabbit pie. Garden. *Bulmer's cider*

MARSTON
Fox Inn
Church Eaton *Wheaton Aston (0785) 840729*
An excellent pub with its own cider bar – or rather barn. Nourishing home-cooked food. Garden. *Weston's cider*

ONECOTE
Jervis Arms
Onecote (053 88) 206
This pretty 17th-century pub stands in the Peak District National Park, and has a lawn running down to the river. Bar food. Normally closed Monday–Wednesday lunchtimes. *Bulmer's cider*

Suffolk

BLYTHBURGH
White Hart
Blythburgh (050 270) 217
A sturdy roadside pub alongside the A12. Excellent selection of food. Vast lawned garden overlooking the River Blyth. *Bulmer's cider*

CAVENDISH
Bull
High Street *Glemsford (0787) 280245*
Good filling food is served in the beamed bar of this appealing old pub. Useful bed and breakfast. Garden. *Bulmer's cider*

IPSWICH
Barwell & Jones (off-licence only)
94, Russhouse Road *Ipswich (0473) 77426*
Aspall cyder

SNAPE
Plough & Sail
The Maltings *Snape (072 888) 413*
Part of the Maltings arts and crafts complex, this rustic pub is a
very popular tourist venue. Bar snacks and meals. *Aspall cyder*

WOODBRIDGE
Barwell & Jones (off-licence only)
2, Church Street *Woodbridge (039 43) 3288*
Aspall cyder

Surrey

FARNCOMBE
Ram Cider House
Catteshall Lane *Godalming (048 68) 21093*
A famous cider house situated in a 16th-century timber-framed
building. Owned by Bulmer's. *Bulmer's cider*

FOREST GREEN
Parrot Inn
Forest Green (030 670) 339
A tile-hung pub overlooking the village green and cricket field.
Bar snacks and restaurant meals. Garden. *Bulmer's cider*

OCKLEY
King's Arms
Stane Street *Dorking (0306) 711224*
Good wholesome food and some excellent local brews bring the
crowds to this immaculate tile-hung pub. Accommodation. Gar-
den. *Merrydown cider*

Sussex (East)

ALFRISTON
Drusillas Valley Wine Cellars
Alfriston (0323) 870234
A rural complex including a zoo, a country park, a crafts centre
and a restaurant. Cider and wine-making exhibitions. *Merry-
down cider*

BLACKBOYS
Blackboys Inn
Framfield (082 582) 283
A well-preserved, centuries-old pub full of cosy beamed rooms.
Food ranges from ploughman's to swordfish steaks. Garden.
Merrydown cider

FIRLE
English Farm Cider Centre (off-licence only)
Middle Farm *Ripe (032 183) 303*
Biddenden cider, Bulmer's cider, Burrow Hill cider (made by
Julian Temperley), *Churchward's cider, Countryman cider,
Dunkerton's cider, Gray's cider, Hill's cider, Inch's cider, Sheppy's
cyder, Symonds' cider, Weston's cider, and others*

Sussex (West)

BILLINGSHURST
Ye Olde Six Bells
76, High Street *Billingshurst (040 381) 2124*
A charming half-timbered pub with the prettiest of gardens, right in the middle of the town. Lunchtime snacks. *Bulmer's cider* (summer only), *Merrydown cider*

FITTLEWORTH
Swan
Fittleworth (079 882) 429
Dating back to the 15th century, this village inn still boasts some original features like a massive inglenook fireplace. Bar snacks and meals. Garden. *Merrydown cider*

ROWHOOK
Chequers Inn
Slinfold (0403) 790480
A delightful old whitewashed pub in the heart of rural Sussex. Light snacks at lunchtime; more elaborate meals in the evening. Garden. *Bulmer's cider*

SCAYNES HILL
Sloop Inn
Freshfield Lane *Scaynes Hill (044 486) 219*
There's a friendly feel to this nice country pub close to the River Ouse. Good nourishing food produced by Jeanne Holland. Garden. *Bulmer's cider*

Warwickshire

HENLEY-IN-ARDEN
Black Swan
23, High Street *Henley-in-Arden (056 42) 2550*
A handsome town-centre hostelry dating back to the 17th century. Bar snacks. Garden. *Bulmer's cider*

NEWBOLD-ON-AVON
Boat
Rugby (0788) 76995
A popular 18th-century pub close by the canal. Bar snacks. Garden. *Weston's cider*

Wiltshire

BRADFORD-ON-AVON
Barge
17, Frome Road *Bradford-on-Avon (022 16) 3403*
A pleasant pub close by the Kennet & Avon canal. Bar food. Garden. *Bulmer's cider*

CHICKSGROVE
Compasses
Fovant (072 270) 318
Farm implements hang on the bare stone walls and a bucolic atmosphere pervades this attractively rustic pub. Bar food and restaurant meals. Garden. *Bulmer's cider*

DEVIZES
Bear Hotel
Market Place *Devizes (0380) 2444*

A fine traditional hostelry dating back some 400 years and still full of character. Interesting bar snacks (look out for the unique Devizes pie – actually a kind of brawn). Good accommodation. *Bulmer's cider*

Yorkshire

HALIFAX
Sportsman Inn
Lee Lane, Shibden *Halifax (0422) 67000*
A very popular pub, fully living up to its name – with a squash court and sauna as added attractions. *Symonds' cider*

SHEFFIELD
Fat Cat
23, Alma Street *Sheffield (0742) 28195*
Popular pub serving home cooked food (good for vegetarians) and offering traditional draught ciders which vary each week: usually one sweet and one dry. Occasionally perry available. Last year they held a cider festival which included 57 varieties of traditional ciders.

SHEFFIELD
Noah's Ark
94, Crookes
A busy, unpretentious little pub, with all the flavour of a true local. *Bulmer's cider*

WALES

Dyfed

NEWCASTLE EMLYN
Pelican Inn
Sycamore Street *Newcastle Emlyn (0239) 710606*
An attractive and nicely preserved beamed pub, including a big
stone hearth with a side oven. Interesting choice of food from
traditional faggots to locally smoked meats. *Weston's cider*

Glamorgan

TREFOREST
Otley Arms
Forest Road *Pontypridd (0443) 402033*
A busy roadside pub offering a good choice of Welsh brews and
cider from across the border. *Thatcher's cider*

Gwent

CHEPSTOW
Castle View Hotel
Bridge Street *Chepstow (029 12) 70349*
Situated across the road from the castle, this friendly, ivy-clad
hotel provides friendly hospitality, tasty food and comfortable
accommodation. Garden. *Bulmer's cider*

WHITEBROOK
Crown at Whitebrook
Monmouth (0600) 860254
More of a restaurant with rooms than a pub, this smartly restored 300-year-old hostelry offers inventive French cooking and excellent accommodation. Closed 1st 2 weeks January. *Weston's cider*

Powys

CRICKHOWELL
Nantyffin Cider Mill Inn
Crickhowell (0873) 810775
A converted cider mill full of history. Cider features in many of the dishes available in the bar, from pork and cider pie to syllabub. Garden. *Bulmer's cider*

LLYSWEN
Griffin Inn
Llyswen (087 485) 241
A pleasant whitewashed pub with its share of exposed stone walls and quarry tiled floors. Excellent accommodation. *Bulmer's cider*

8
CIDER
IN THE KITCHEN

CIDER is meant for drinking, but it also belongs in the kitchen where it can improve and add interest to all kinds of dishes. In its way it is as useful and versatile as wine.

Cider is, first of all, an excellent marinade, helping to tenderize tough meat; it is also a preservative, so it can be added to pickles and used for sousing fish. In fact it complements fish superbly and is the natural ingredient for sauces to go with mackerel, roast conger eel and the like. Cider provides a tart foil to the fattiness of pork and other rich meats, and goes perfectly with joints of bacon and ham. You can also use it to brighten up dull vegetables, enrich stews and casseroles and add an extra dimension to bland cakes and puddings.

There is no such thing as 'cooking cider', but as a general rule you should use draught or good-quality bottled cider in recipes. Dry or medium-sweet brands are the most suitable, although you can always experiment with different types. Fizzy bottled and keg ciders are not so good for cooking; they create a great deal of effervescence, but have little depth of flavour. And it is the flavour which is important; the better the cider, the better the resulting dish.

When you add cider to a dish and cook it, the alcohol evaporates, leaving only the fruitiness and sharpness of the apples. Always add cider at room temperature or slightly warm; if you pour it in ice-cold from the fridge much of the flavour will be lost.

The following recipes are arranged in conventional menu order,

98

beginning with soups and starters and ending with puddings.
Unless otherwise stated, all recipes are for four people. Follow
either the imperial *or* the metric measurements; don't try to mix
the two.

Mussel and Cider Soup

Mussels are in season from September to April, and this creamy, saffron-tinged soup makes an exquisite start to a winter meal.

2 dozen mussels
1 small leek
1 onion
½ pt (300ml) cider
½ pt (300ml) water
pinch of saffron
1 tablespoon each of chopped fresh parsley and chives
¼ pt (150ml) single cream
salt and pepper to taste

Clean the mussels carefully, removing their 'beards' and discarding any that are damaged or half-open. Put in a large pan, along with the chopped leek, onion, saffron, water and cider. Bring to the boil and cook until the mussels just open. Don't overcook otherwise they will become leathery. Strain and reserve the stock. Remove the mussels from their shells.

Warm the stock in a separate pan, stir in the cream and adjust the seasoning. Add the mussels, toss in the freshly chopped herbs and serve.

Onion and Cider Soup

A variation on the theme of French onion soup.

1 lb (450g) onions
2 oz (50g) butter
½ pt (300ml) cider
1 ½ pts (900ml) beef stock
salt and pepper to taste
1 tablespoon cornflour

Peel and thinly slice the onions. Melt the butter in a large saucepan and cook the onions gently for about 15 minutes until they are soft and golden-brown. Pour in the cider and the beef stock (this can be made from a stock cube if necessary). Season with salt and pepper, bring to the boil, then simmer with a lid on for 30 minutes. Finally blend the cornflour with a little water and stir into the soup.

Serve piping hot with crisp, cheese-topped croûtons.

Serves four – six

Pigeon Breast Salad

A recipe created by Christopher Oakes, one of the new breed of inventive young English chefs. It has all the subtlety and refinement of French *nouvelle cuisine*.

1 pigeon breast, boned and skinned
1 oz (25g) butter
1 tablespoon cider vinegar (or equal parts cider and white wine vinegar)
3 tablespoons walnut oil
salt and pepper
a few leaves of radicchio, curly endive, corn salad and oak-leaf lettuce
1 oz (25g) finely diced bacon
a few pine kernels
1 blanched tomato

Season the pigeon breast and shallow fry in butter, leaving it still pink.

Make a dressing with the cider vinegar, walnut oil and salt and pepper.

Arrange the seasoned salad leaves around a plate. The red of the radicchio (Italian red lettuce) contrasts with the greens of the other leaves.

Fry the diced bacon until crisp, add the pine kernels. Remove the pan from the heat and add the dressing to slightly warm it.

Slice the pigeon breast into six. Arrange on top of the salad. Decorate with strips of tomato flesh and cover with the warm dressing.

Serves one

Somerset Rarebit

The West Country's answer to Welsh rarebit, made with cider rather than beer.

½ oz (12g) butter
8 oz (225g) Cheddar cheese
2 fl oz (60ml) cider
1 teaspoon Worcestershire sauce
1 teaspoon prepared English mustard
salt and pepper
4 slices buttered toast

Melt the butter in the pan and stir in the grated cheese. Blend well over a low heat until the cheese is melted. Add the cider, Worcestershire sauce, mustard, salt and pepper. Pour the mixture, piping hot, over buttered toast, put under the grill to brown and serve straight away as the topping bubbles.

Chicken Brawn

Brawn is usually made from a pig's head. This is a more delicate version, ideal for a cold luncheon or supper. The pig's trotters in the recipe help to provide the rich jellied stock that binds the pieces of meat together.

3 lb(1 ½kg) boiling fowl
2 pig's trotters
salt and pepper
bundle of mixed herbs
cider
2 hard-boiled eggs

Truss the fowl and put it into a large saucepan with the pig's trotters, salt, pepper and a bundle of mixed herbs of your choice (tarragon, parsley, bay leaves, etc.). Cover with cider, bring to the boil, then turn down the heat and simmer very slowly for 4 hours with the lid on. Strain the stock, put to one side and leave the chicken and trotters to cool.

Remove the meat from the chicken, discarding any skin and fat, and chop finely. Any lean meat on the trotters can be chopped up too. Return to the stock and heat through. Line a mould with sliced hard-boiled eggs, pour in the meat and stock and leave to cool. Press under a weight for several hours, and cool in the fridge. Turn out when set and serve in slices.

Casseroled Chicken with Apricots

4 oz (100g) dried apricots
3 lb (1½kg) chicken
¼ pt (150ml) cider
2 tablespoons honey
2 tablespoons butter
salt and pepper

Wash the dried apricots well and allow them to soak in cold water overnight.

Next day cut the chicken in four and marinate in cider for 2 hours. Remove the chicken (reserve the cider) and dry thoroughly. Mix together the honey and butter over a low heat, and spread generously over the chicken. Keep back about 1 tablespoon of the mixture.

Pour the cider marinade into a casserole dish and add the apricots and chicken. Season and cook in a moderate oven at 350°F (180°C), Gas Mark 4, for about 45 minutes. Remove the chicken pieces and place on a grilling rack. Brush with the rest of the honey and butter, and grill until golden brown. Serve with the apricots and cider sauce.

Roast Leg of Lamb with Honey and Cider Sauce

1 leg of lamb
salt
2 tablespoons honey
1 oz (25g) butter
¼ pt (150ml) cider
sprigs of rosemary

Rub the joint with a little salt. Melt the butter in a saucepan and stir in the honey and the cider; blend well. Brush this mixture over the meat so that it is well covered. Then with a sharp pointed knife make a number of little incisions into the meat, and insert a small sprig of rosemary into each one.

Put the joint in a roasting tin, cover with foil and cook at 350°F (180°F), Gas Mark 4, allowing 25 minutes per lb. (450g) plus 25 minutes. Baste from time to time.

Spoon the juices over the meat once it has been carved.

Lamp Chops with Mint and Lemon Sauce

4 chump chops
flour
salt and pepper
1 oz (25g) butter
1 tablespoon olive oil
rind and juice of 1 lemon
1 ½ tablespoons chopped fresh mint
6 tablespoons cider
watercress to garnish

Dip the chops in seasoned flour. Melt the butter with the oil in a frying pan until really hot. Add the chops and cook over a low heat for 5–7 minutes each side (depending on thickness). Drain the chops on kitchen paper, arrange on a serving dish and keep warm.

Add the lemon juice, thinly sliced rind, chopped mint and cider to the pan juices. Bring to the boil, stirring well, and cook for 2 minutes until nicely reduced. Pour over the chops, garnish with sprigs of watercress and serve with redcurrant jelly.

Gammon in Cider

Gammon is the most princely of all bacon joints, but this recipe is equally good with cheaper cuts such as collar. It also works well with salted belly of pork.

3 lb (1 ½kg) piece of gammon
1 carrot
1 onion
1 teaspoon cloves
1 teaspoon black peppercorns
1 bay leaf
cider

GLAZE:
1 tablespoon Dijon mustard
1 heaped tablespoon redcurrant jelly
juice of 1 orange
1 tablespoon brown sugar

Soak the gammon in water for a few hours to remove excess saltiness. Drain and place in a saucepan with the carrot, onion, herbs, spices and enough cider to cover the joint. Bring to the boil then simmer gently for 1¼ hours.

Remove the gammon and allow to cool slightly. Peel off the skin and score the fat diagonally into diamond shapes. Mix together the ingredients of the glaze and spread over the surface of the meat. Put the joint into a hot oven 400°F (200°C), Gas Mark 6, for 15 minutes, basting well, until the glaze is a rich golden colour.

Serve with pease pudding, green vegetables, new potatoes and a purée of apples or apricots.

Pheasant Casseroled in Cider

Casseroling is an ideal way of dealing with game birds of all kinds, especially those that are old. It produces a rich, full-flavoured dish. Equally good with pigeon and grouse, and also a delicious method of cooking rabbit.

2 pheasants
flour
8 oz (225g) button onions
3 tablespoons oil
¾ pt (450ml) cider
grated rind and juice of 1 orange
1 tablespoon redcurrant jelly
8 oz (225g) fresh/tinned chestnuts
salt and pepper
chopped parsley to garnish

Split the pheasants in two along the backbone and roll in flour. Heat the oil in a large pan and fry the pheasants and whole button onions until slightly browned. Put into a large casserole dish that will easily contain the birds.

Add the cider, orange rind and juice, and redcurrant jelly to the pan juices, bring to the boil and simmer for 2 minutes, stirring well. Pour over the pheasants.

Peel and skin the chestnuts (if fresh) and add to the casserole. (If using tinned chestnuts, add half an hour before end of cooking.) Adjust the seasoning, cover and cook in the oven at 350°F (180°C), Gas Mark 4, for about 1½ hours until the pheasants are really tender. (Cooking time will vary with the age of the birds: old ones take longer.)

Garnish with chopped parsley and serve.

Sausages in Cider

This robust dish is best made with meaty, good-quality butchers' sausages rather than insipid factory-produced concoctions.

8 thick pork sausages
1 onion
½ pt(300ml) cider
1 apple
1 tablespoon chopped sage
salt and pepper

Fry the sausages in a little butter or dripping for 5 minutes until they firm up. Remove from the pan and transfer to an ovenproof dish. Fry the onion in the fat from the sausages until coloured, then pour in the cider and swirl round the pan.

Peel, core and slice the apple into rings and arrange over the sausages. Sprinkle with sage, season with salt and pepper and pour in the cider juices and onion. Cook in a moderate oven at 325°F (170°C), Gas Mark 3, for about 30 minutes, although longer cooking does no harm to this dish.

Serve with heaps of mashed potatoes and fresh tomato sauce.

Squab Pie

Squab was the old West Country name for a young pigeon, and this delicious fruity pie was originally made with pigeon. Over the years that has been replaced by lamb or mutton, but the pies are as excellent as ever.

1 lb (450g) lean lamb or mutton
1 lb (450g) onions
1 lb (450g) crisp cooking apples
a pinch of nutmeg and a pinch of cinnamon
2 tablespoons brown sugar
¼ pt (150ml) stock
¼ pt (150ml) cider
salt and pepper
8 oz (225g) shortcrust pastry

Trim the meat and cut into small cubes; peel and slice the onions; peel, core and slice the apples.

Put a layer of apples at the bottom of a greased pie dish, and sprinkle with a little spice and sugar. Then add a layer of meat and a layer of onions. Repeat until all the ingredients are used up. Season with salt and pepper, and pour in the stock and cider.

Moisten the edges of the pie dish with water and put on the pastry lid, pressing the edges down well. Brush with a little beaten egg or milk. Bake in a moderate oven at 350°F (180°C), Gas Mark 4, for 45 minutes.

This pie was traditionally eaten with clotted cream.

Whiting with Grapes

A simple recipe which is equally good with grey mullet, mackerel or sea bass, as well as whiting.

4 whiting (about 8 oz (225g) each)
2 oz (50g) olive oil
a sprig of thyme
1 bay leaf
3 tablespoons cider
12 seedless white grapes
slices of lemon to garnish

Arrange the cleaned and gutted fish in a shallow fireproof dish. Pour oil over them, add the herbs, cider and a little salt and pepper. Bake, uncovered for 15 minutes at 350°F (180°C), Gas Mark 4. Toss in the white grapes and cook for a further 5 minutes.

Serve in their own juice, with slices of lemon decorating each fish.

Salmon en Pain de Caudebec

Salmon loaf from Caudebec

A splendid summer dish from Caudebec in the cider-producing region of north-west France. Adapted from a recipe in Alan Davidson's excellent *North Atlantic Seafood* (Macmillan, 1979).

1 ½ lb (675g) fresh salmon (a tail piece is ideal)
1 lb (450g) potatoes
1 tablespoon each of finely chopped fresh parsley,
tarragon and chives
2 shallots
2 oz (50g) butter
4 tablespoons dry cider
1 tablespoon calvados (optional)
½ pt (300ml) single cream
salt and pepper

Poach the salmon in slightly salted water or stock for about 7 minutes. Boil the potatoes, mash them and mix with 2 tablespoons of the mixed herbs, finely chopped shallots and butter.

Skin the salmon, flake it and add to the mashed potato mixture. Moisten with cider and calvados (if you have some). Grease a mould with butter, put in the salmon mixture and press down lightly. Chill for 6–12 hours. When you are ready to serve the dish, lower the mould into very hot water for a minute, then invert it. Serve the salmon loaf with a jug of cream seasoned with salt and pepper and the remainder of the fresh herbs. Garnish with slices of lemon.

Serves six

Soused Mackerel

A traditional West Country recipe, combining the region's most abundant fish with its most famous drink. Equally good with herrings.

4 mackerel
1 onion
1 tablespoon fresh parsley, chopped
4 bay leaves
1 teaspoon cloves
1 teaspoon black peppercorns
sprig of fresh fennel
pinch of salt
¼ pt (150ml) cider
¼ pt (150ml) white vinegar

Gut, clean and behead the mackerel and lay them in an ovenproof dish. Add the chopped onion, parsley, bay leaves, cloves and peppercorns. Pour over the cider and vinegar, top with a sprig of fresh fennel and bake in the oven at 350°F (180°C), Gas Mark 4, for 45 minutes.

Remove from the oven and allow to cool for several hours before serving. Eat with crusty bread or potato salad.

Baked Onions

The addition of cider gives this simple dish a touch of class.

4 large onions
5 fl oz (150ml) cider
1 fl oz (30ml) white wine vinegar
2 tablespoons water
salt and pepper
2 rashers streaky bacon

Peel the onions and place in a greased ovenproof dish. Add the cider, wine vinegar and water, season with salt and pepper and bake at 350°F (180°C), Gas Mark 4, for about 1 hour, or until the onions are soft. You may need to add a little extra water during cooking if the dish appears to be drying out.

Fry the rashers of bacon, cut into small pieces and scatter over the onions just before serving.

Glazed Parsnips

The sharp, fruity flavour of the cider balances the sweetness of
the parsnips in this simple, but effective, American recipe.

6 medium parsnips
2 oz (50g) butter
2 oz (50g) brown sugar
¼ pt (150ml) cider
1 teaspoon salt

Peel the parsnips, cut in quarters lengthwise and cut out any
woody core. Cook in salted water until just tender. Drain well.
Lay in a shallow baking dish.

Blend together the butter and sugar and add the cider and salt.
Spoon this mixture over the parsnips. Bake for 15 minutes at
400°F (200°C), Gas Mark 6, basting occasionally with the glaze.

Baked Red Cabbage

1 medium-sized red cabbage
1 oz (25g) butter
¼ pt (150ml) cider
2 tablespoons white wine vinegar
1 lb (450g) cooking apples
1 tablespoon brown sugar

Put the shredded cabbage into an earthenware dish, along with the butter, cider and wine vinegar. Cover and cook in the oven at 350°F (180°C), Gas Mark 4, for 30 minutes. Add the peeled and chopped apples and the sugar, and cook for a further 30 minutes at the same temperature, until the cabbage is soft and tender.

A perfect accompaniment to rich roast meats like pork.

Serves six

Pickled French Beans

An unusual recipe if you have a surplus of French beans in the garden.

1 lb (450g) French beans
¼ pt (150ml) dry cider
¼ pt (150ml) white vinegar
4 oz (100g) brown sugar
2 teaspoons dill seeds
¼ teaspoon turmeric
¼ teaspoon cayenne pepper

Choose beans that are firm and fresh, but not too large. Top and tail them, and boil in salted water for 5 minutes, ensuring that they remain crisp. Do not overcook, otherwise they will become mushy in the pickle. Drain well and pack carefully into a large jar.

Meanwhile put all the other ingredients in a saucepan with the cider and vinegar, and boil for 10 minutes. Then pour the hot, spiced vinegar over the beans, making sure they are completely covered. Seal the jar and leave for at least a month before opening.

Apple and Mint Chutney

A dash of cider helps to enhance the sharp fruity flavour of this chutney.

2 lbs (900g) cooking apples
1 lb (450g) onions
8 oz (225g) tomatoes
4 oz (100g) stoned raisins
2 teaspoons finely chopped mint
2 teaspoons salt
1 teaspoon dry mustard powder
1 teaspoon cayenne pepper
8 oz (225g) soft brown sugar
¼ pt (150ml) cider
1 pt (600ml) malt vinegar

First prepare all the ingredients: peel and chop the apples, tomatoes and onions; chop the raisins and mint. Put into a preserving pan with the cider and half the vinegar and cook slowly until soft. Meanwhile mix the mustard and cayenne pepper with a little of the remaining vinegar and add to the pan. When all the ingredients are soft, stir in the sugar, salt and the rest of the vinegar, and boil until the chutney is thick (approximately 30 minutes). Allow to cool slightly, then pot and cover.

Store for at least six months before opening. Keeps well and improves with age.

Syllabub

Traditionally syllabub was made by milking the cow direct into a bucket of cider, sweetening the frothy mixture and serving immediately. In the absence of a cow, this is how you might do it today.

juice and rind of ½ lemon
¼ pt (150ml) cider
1 tablespoon brandy
2 oz (50g) caster sugar
¾ pt (450ml) double cream

Grate the lemon rind finely and squeeze out the juice. Put into a bowl with the cider, brandy and sugar and stir well until the sugar is completely dissolved. Pour in the cream, whisk briskly. Spoon into individual tall glasses, and serve with wafer biscuits or brandy snaps.

Cider and Peach Water Ice

4 oz (100g) sugar
½ pt (300ml) water
juice and rind of 1 lemon
½ pt (300ml) cider
2 peaches, peeled, stoned and chopped
white of 1 egg

Dissolve the sugar in water over a low heat, bring to the boil and cook for 10 minutes. Add lemon rind and juice and allow to cool. Strain. Add the cider to the syrup and pour into a shallow dish. Place in the freezer compartment of the fridge until the mixture just begins to freeze. Remove, turn the mixture into a bowl, fold in the whisked egg white and the chopped peaches. Mix thoroughly, return to the dish and freeze.

Apple and Banana Surprise

The surprise here is the layer of sliced bananas hidden beneath the apples.

1 lb (450g) cooking apples
2 oz (50g) sugar
2 oz (50g) sultanas
4 tablespoons cider
2 bananas
4 oz (100g) breadcrumbs
2 or 3 knobs of butter

Peel, core and slice the apples, and stew in a saucepan with the sugar, sultanas and cider until soft and pulpy. Grease an oven-proof dish and put a layer of sliced bananas at the bottom of it. Cover with stewed apples and top with breadcrumbs. Dot with two or three knobs of butter and bake at 375°F (190°C), Gas Mark 5, for 15 minutes.

Serve hot with rich, thick, clotted cream.

Stewed Apples with Quinces

Stewed apple has no great reputation as a dessert, but here it is transformed with fragrant quinces, fruity cider and sweet heather honey.

1 ½ lbs (675g) cooking apples
8 oz (225g) quinces
4 oz (100g) sugar
½ pint (300ml) cider
4 cloves
1 cinnamon stick
juice of ½ lemon
strip of lemon or orange peel
1 oz (25g) heather honey

Peel, core and slice the apples and quinces. Put in a pan with the sugar, cider, spices, lemon juice and peel. Cook gently until the fruit is soft, but not mushy. Remove the spices and peel, and stir in the honey.

Serve warm or cold with cream.

Serves six

Samson

A powerful, strong drink from Cornwall. It can be put into bottles and served from time to time in small wine glasses.

1 pt (600ml) cider
½ pt (300ml) rum
honey to taste

Warm the cider for an hour, add the rum and allow to get cold. Store in bottles. Serve as a warming nip, sweetening to taste.

Mulled Cider

Just the drink for wassailing your friends at Christmas!

2 pt (1.2 litres) cider
4 oz (100g) sugar
12 cloves
4 sticks cinnamon
12 whole allspice berries

Warm the cider in a large pan and stir in the sugar with a wooden spoon. Add the spices. Simmer gently until the sugar is completely dissolved and the cider is hot and spicy. Serve at once.

Cider Punch

4 pt (2½ litres) cider
3 fl oz (100ml) brandy
2 oranges
6 cloves
2 dessert apples
pice of lemon peel
brown sugar to taste

Warm the cider and brandy in a large pan; stick the oranges with cloves, and slice the apples; add oranges and apples to the pan, along with the lemon peel and sufficient brown sugar to taste. Simmer for 20 minutes before serving.

Poor Man's Black Velvet

Traditionally made with Guinness and champagne, but a very acceptable, and cheaper, substitute is Guinness with an equal quantity of dry vintage cider.

Poor Man's Bucks Fizz

Sparkling vintage cider again replaces champagne in this classic drink. Chill the cider well and then add fresh orange juice (about half and half, depending on your taste).

9

CIDER VINEGAR
AND CIDER DISTILLED

Cider Vinegar

A MIRACULOUS CURE

THE medicinal virtues of drinking cider have been extolled for hundreds of years (see page 8), but they are mild compared with the extravagant claims made for cider vinegar. These date from 1948, when the English composer and mystic, Cyril Scott, published a little book entitled simply *Cider Vinegar*; in the 1960s a certain Dr DeForest Clinton Jarvis of the University of Vermont spread the word with the zeal of an evangelist. His books *Folk Medicine* and *Arthritis and Folk Medicine*, which became world bestsellers, were based on the ancient folk remedies of the mountain villagers of Vermont, and Jarvis built around his findings a new theory of medicine. He believed that the doctor should also be a teacher and explained the healthiness of the Vermont people – who lived in one of the most climatically unstable regions in the world – in two ways: that they maintained the correct acid balance and ensured the right mineral content in the blood (potassium was particularly important).

The vital weapon in his armoury was cider vinegar, which he saw as a panacea, a cure-all for everything from arthritis, obesity and kidney troubles to headaches and hiccups. He was also convinced that cider vinegar was the best way of keeping the body in good working order, thereby preventing disease. More recently the cause has been taken up by Maurice Hannsen (see Bibliography).

MAKING CIDER VINEGAR

Leave cider exposed to the air for long enough and it turns to vinegar, thanks to a micro-organism called *Acetobacter*. In practice, the vinegar fly is the most effective agent for turning cider into vinegar. Of course on a commercial scale the process has to be much more carefully organized and controlled. There are four main producers in England: Whiteways, Aspall and Merrydown (who market cider vinegar under the trade name Martlet) are all cider-makers in their own right; Applefords of Colnbrook, Slough, also specialize in cider vinegar.

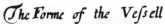

The Forme of the Vessell

a - *The Bung hole.*
b - *a small vent hole.*
c - *the Tap.*

A 'stund' or vessel for storing cider in the 17th century.

Different cider-makers use slightly different technical processes, but the principle is always the same. Matured cider is put into huge vats and a fine suspension of air bubbles and fermenting liquid is passed through it. The oxygen in the air bubbles causes the *Acetobacter* to grow and turn the alcohol in the cider into vinegar. This is then siphoned off and bottled.

Cider vinegar is produced without any additives or preservatives; it is light, clear and straw coloured – although it may darken once it has been opened.

AT HOME

A very passable cider vinegar can be made at home without resorting to the technology employed by the commercial cider makers. In an emergency you can simply mix together equal quantities of dry cider and white (distilled) vinegar. Larger quantities can be prepared by putting 4 oz (100g) sugar in a half-gallon container and adding 3 pints (1½ litres) dry cider plus ¼ pint (150ml) distilled vinegar. Cover with a piece of clean cloth, tie down securely and leave for 3–4 months.

THE VIRTUES OF CIDER VINEGAR

The effectiveness of cider vinegar can be explained by its constituents. It is very rich in minerals, particularly potassium, and has a lot of organic acid, so it helps combat any alkaline reaction in the blood due to stress or processed foods, and it helps the body to eliminate fat rather than allowing it to be stored.

For those embarking on the treatment for the first time, the experts recommend one or two teaspoons of cider vinegar mixed in a tumbler of cold or warm water. Take one glass in the morning, one during or after lunch and one in the evening.

Even more efficacious is 'oxymel', a blend of cider vinegar and unpasteurized honey, which is listed in the *British Pharmaco-*

poeia and has been used in medicine for centuries. It is a bittersweet and refreshing drink produced by Merrydown under the name of Honegar; it has been recommended for hay fever and asthma, and soothes coughs. Honey also helps the absorption of cider vinegar and makes it easier on the stomach.

CULINARY USES

For those who like to take their medicine less clinically, there are a great many ways of using cider vinegar in cooking. It can be used as an alternative to both wine vinegar and malt vinegar for pickling; it can be flavoured with herbs of all kinds and is delicious with fish and chips. It gives a distinctive flavour to salad dressings, mustard and sauces; and, like cider, it is an effective marinade.

Cider distilled

In *Vinetum Britannicum*, John Worlidge recommended that the English should distil cider to produce a spirit that would oust expensive foreign brandy. The challenge was taken up by one Richard Haines of Sullington in Sussex who, in 1684, took out a patent for what he called Cider Royal. In his words it was 'an art or method of preparing, improving and meliorating cyder, perry and the juice of liquors of wilding crabbs so as to put the strength or goodness of two or three hogsheads into one and render the same much more wholesome and delightful.' And this is how he did it: 'Put one hogshead of cyder into a copper still and then put the same into your other hogshead and fill it up, stirr it about well and keep it close stopt except one day in ten or twenty let it lie open five or six hours. Within three months this will be as strong as the best French wines and as pleasing – though different in taste.' Using this method he could produce a pint of spirit from every gallon of cider.

If this seemed like hard work, there was, in the opinion of many 17th-century cider-makers, a much simpler way. They erroneously believed that if cider was bottled and left to mature, it would spontaneously turn into spirit or *aqua vitae*; 'the bottles smoak at the opening, and it catches flame speedily, and will burn like spirit of wine, with a fiery taste'. So said Doctor John Beale, who wrote a treatise on cider and also had some knowledge of distilling cider.

But the fashion for Cider Royal didn't last, despite the claim that a man could be 'fuddled' and sober twice a day with it and suffer no 'mischief to his health'! It was left to the French to perfect the distillation of apples and cider, from which they created one of the finest of all spirits, calvados.

CALVADOS

The calvados region of Normandy takes its name from that of a Spanish galleon, *El Calvador*, wrecked off the coast while fleeing from Sir Francis Drake's flotilla. Apple brandy has been made in the area since the middle of the 16th century when a certain Sieur de Gouberville commissioned the local blacksmith at Mesnil-au-Val on the Cotentin peninsula to build him a still so that he could make brandy from apples. The name calvados wasn't applied to the spirit until after the French Revolution; now there are eleven distinct areas, each producing its own brand.

Since 1946 there have been strict regulations governing the production and quality of calvados, and only one type – that produced in the Pays d'Auge area – is *appellation contrôlée*. To earn this seal of approval, the calvados has to be made from fruit crushed in the traditional manner and fermented for at least one month; it must be distilled twice in a pot-still like cognac and must be matured for at least one year. In practice the best calvados is matured for 6–10 years in great oak vats before it is bottled and sold. Young calvados is like firewater, but age brings a mellowness and a heady apple perfume.

Eau de vie de cidre is a rougher spirit altogether, produced cheaply in some parts of rural Normandy. It can be made in a continuous still, but it can't be called calvados.

Butter, cream and calvados are the three ingredients which give Normandy cuisine its characteristic flavour and richness. And it's the calvados which helps to balance out the other two, providing a sharp edge and aroma, particularly in sauces for pork, veal, chicken and game.

There is a tradition of drinking a glass of calvados between courses in a heavy meal, to make a hole – or *trou normand*; this cleans the palate, helps digestion and paves the way for the next course.

APPLEJACK

Cider has been brewed and drunk in the apple-growing regions of the USA since the 18th century, and there they make an apple spirit called 'applejack', or more colourfully 'essence of lockjaw'. It is made in a similar way to calvados: distilled twice in a pot still, diluted and aged in oak casks for up to five years.

10
APPLE JUICE
AND APPLE WINE

THE juice from true cider apples is undrinkable before it has been fermented; however dessert and culinary apples yield a most pleasant beverage when crushed. Most cider-makers are content to produce cider and nothing else, but a few, especially in the south and east, market apple juice as a sideline.

John Chevallier Guild, at the Aspall Cyder House, Stowmarket, Suffolk, produces some of the finest apple juice in the land from organically grown fruit. The best quality apples are crushed, then the juice is pasteurized and bottled. It's as simple as that. No apples from cold storage are used, as this tends to impair the flavour and quality of the juice.

Merrydown at Horam, Sussex, also produce apple juice in conjunction with cider-making. They use a blend of mainly Bramleys and Coxes for their juice, but do add ascorbic acid (vitamin C) to prevent oxidation. Biddenden Vineyards in Kent also make apple juice as part of their operation.

But not all apple juice comes from the cider-makers. Fruit farmers like James White at Istana Orchard, Cratfield, Suffolk, produces a range of apple juices, two made from specific varieties of apple – Russet and Cox – and a third from a blend of varieties. And he adds nothing in the way of artificial colouring or preservatives to them. The same goes for Devorah Peake at Hill Farm, near Colchester, where some 1 million bottles of Copella apple juice are produced each year from Cox's Orange Pippins.

MAKING APPLE JUICE AT HOME

First you will need a supply of apples in good condition. Go for the classic dessert varieties like Cox's Orange Pippins and Russets, supplemented by a small quantity of Bramleys if you want a sharply flavoured juice. Prepare and crush the fruit as described on page 36 and strain it through muslin to remove any big bits of partially crushed apple. Don't attempt to filter it or strain it finely so that it becomes clear, since most of the nutrients are contained in the fine suspension of pulp and juice. Some people recommend that you add, say, half a teaspoon of ascorbic acid to each gallon of juice to help prevent oxidation.

If you wish you can store the fresh juice in the freezer, but it's probably more convenient to bottle it. Use old screw-top beer or cider bottles, preferably of dark glass. Clean them well and fill them with the juice, leaving a little space at the neck of the bottle.

Next, you will have to sterilize the bottles. Put the caps on loosely and put the bottles upright into a large pan of water using some kind of trivet or false bottom to keep them out of direct contact with the pan. Make sure the water level comes up to the neck of the bottles. You can use newspaper padding to keep each bottle apart and upright.

Bring to the boil and simmer at 190°F (90°C) for 20 minutes, topping up with hot water if the level begins to drop. When sterilization is complete, remove the bottles (remember they will be very hot, so use an oven cloth), tighten the caps and leave until cool. Store in a cool place away from the light.

Apple wine

In the golden cider-making days of the 17th century, cider was regarded as a wine because it had similar qualities and character.

Nowadays, apple wine is a distinct product in its own right and a number of cider-makers, including Merrydown, Biddenden Vineyards and Symonds' produce it (sometimes as part of a whole range of so-called English country wines).

There are also a few wine-makers producing apple wine alongside the grape variety. One of the best known is Robin Don, who has a vineyard at Elmham Park, near Dereham, Norfolk. He ferments apple juice 'with all the care that one gives to a fine white wine', often using supplies from Devorah Peake at Hill Farm, near Colchester, whose Copella apple juice is highly regarded (see page 132).

The elaborate processes involved in making apple wine – the fermentation with special yeast, the addition of sugar, racking, filtering and bottling, are really outside the scope of this book, but interested readers who want to make their own should consult one of the many specialist books available, such as *Home Brewing and Wine-Making* by W.H.T. Tayleur (Penguin, 1973).

11

PERRY

Of Peres, wyne is made, if they be grounde
And through a rare sack with fors y wronge . . .
Of pears, sour and wild, it is no wronge
Aysell (vinegar) to bringe . . .

MAKING a drink from hard, gritty wild pears was clearly nothing new to the Roman writer Palladius (here interpreted by a medieval scholar). Like crab apples they were impossible to eat, but could be transformed by crushing and fermentation. Perry is made in exactly the same way as cider.

The word 'perry' comes from the Old English *pirige*, meaning pear tree, and it appears in a number of English place names in counties as far apart as Kent, Oxfordshire and Staffordshire. After the Anglo-Saxons colonized England they named many of their settlements after features in the countryside, so these names probably celebrate outstanding wild pear trees or even established orchards.

When the Romans arrived in Britain, they not only brought with them cider and cider apples, but also many kinds of perry pear.

During the Middle Ages it was the custom to sell 'piriwhit', a kind of 'small perry' diluted with water or cheap ale, to labourers and people living alone who could not brew their own. But perry never achieved the popularity or reputation of its apple-based relative and was generally cheaper. It was very much the poor relation.

THE NAMING OF PEARS

Perry pear trees were renowned not only for their great size but also for their longevity; there's a saying that 'He that planteth perry pears truly planteth for his heirs.' Indeed on the banks of the River Wye near Holme Lacy, Herefordshire, there are still some rooted branches of a great tree which, in 1790, was said to cover three-quarters of an acre and yield 5–7 tons of fruit each year.

Another advantage of perry pear trees was the fact that they would grow successfully in 'common fields, gravelly, wild and stony ground', and soils that were too poor to support cider apples. One famous 17th-century pear was actually called Bare Land because it thrived in barren ground.

Like cider apples, perry pears had colourful descriptive names. The Long Ashton Research Station has recorded over 100 different varieties with some 200 local names – since the same pear might have different names in different districts. The great perry pears of the 17th century included, as well as the Bare Land, the Red Squash, the Green Squash, the Mary Pear, the Drake Pear and the John Pear; then there was the Thorn Pear, and the ancient Red Pear, dating back to Tudor times and looking more like a ripe red apple. In more modern times the Oldfield and Yellow Huffcap (an immense tree even by pear standards) have been popular with perry-makers.

There were lots of nicknames too: Merrylegs or Mumblehead obviously had a potent reputation; Ironsides was hard as iron, while the Swan Egg and Potato Pear presumably did not look much like pears at all.

DECLINE AND FALL

By the end of the 18th century many of the great trees planted during the 15th and 16th centuries were coming to the end of their natural life, and there was no systematic planting to replace them. Commercial production faltered, the weather often caused the pear crop to fail and perry-making became less and less popular. In its heyday, perry had been made from the juice of a single variety because the fruit was so plentiful; now the juice from different varieties had to be blended to produce a worthwhile amount of perry.

But even in the early years of this century, important cidermakers were still producing some perry. In their 1913 catalogue, Whiteways of Whimple listed two types – Oldfield and Barland – both named after classic perry pears. Nowadays most perry is produced around the Wye Valley and the Severn: Weston's of Much Marcle, near Ledbury, Hereford, and W.R. Symonds at Stoke Lacy, Bromyard, Hereford, are the two major producers. Perry can be obtained on draught or in bottles, but is not widely distributed. A number of firms, including Bulmer's and Coates Gaymers also produce sparkling pear-based drinks, but these bear little resemblance to traditional perry.

Perry is still very much a rarity, but with the revival of interest in traditional cider and the planting of new perry pear orchards in Somerset, it could be set for a comeback. Sample it if you can and you will discover it is very different in character from cider; it has a much yellower colour and a rather rich, thick flavour. But be warned: it has a devastatingly purgative effect.

Bibliography

HISTORICAL

Lawson, William. *A New Orchard and Garden*, 1648

Evelyn, John. *Pomona* (part of a larger work *Sylva*), 1664. (This also contains *General Advertisements Concerning Cider* by Dr J. Beale; Sir Paul Neil's *Discourse of Cider*; *Observations Concerning the Making and Preserving of Cider* by John Newburgh; *Concerning Cider* by Doctor Smith; *Of Cider* by Captain Sylas Taylor; *An Account of Perry and Cider Out of Glosestershire* imparted by Daniel Collwall; *For Making of Cider* out of Mr Cook; *Another Account of Cider from a Person of Great Experience*)

Worlidge, John. *Vinetum Britannicum*, 1676

Haines, R. *Aphorisms on the New Way of Improving Cyder*, 1684

Worlidge, John. *The Most Easie Method of Making the Best Cyder*, 1687

Philips, John. *Cyder, A Poem*, 1708

Ellis, W. *The Compleat Cyderman*, 1754

Stafford, H. *A Treatise on Cyder-Making*, 1759

Knight, T.A. *A Treatise on the Culture of the Apple and Pear and on the Manufacture of Cider and Perry*, 1809

Ham, J. *The Manufacture of Cider and Perry Reduced to Rules*, 1828

Bull, H.G. & Hogg, R. (ed). *The Herefordshire Pomona*, 1876–1885

Stopes, H. *Cider: The History, Method of Manufacture and Properties of this National Beverage*, 1888

Radcliffe-Cooke, C.W. *A Book about Cider and Perry*, 1898

BIBLIOGRAPHY

GENERAL

Berry, Mary. *Cider for All Seasons* (Woodhead-Faulkner, Cambridge, 1977)

Carr, J.G. *Modern Methods of Cider Making* (National Association of Cider Makers, n.d.)

Cider (National Association of Cider Makers, 1980)

Deal, Jo. *Making Cider* (Amateur Winemaker Publications, 1976)

French, R.K. *The History and Virtues of Cider* (Robert Hale, London, 1982)

Hanssen, Maurice. *Hanssen's Complete Cider Vinegar* (Thorsons, Wellingborough, 1979)

Harrison, Shirley. *A Taste of Cider* (David & Charles, Newton Abbot, 1982)

Quinion, Michael B. *A Drink for its Time* (Museum of Cider, 1979)

Quinion, Michael B. *Cidermaking* (Shire Publications, Princes Risborough, 1982)

Scott, Cyril. *Cider Vinegar* (Athene, 1948; reprinted 1984)

Turner, Ben. *Home Brewed Beer and Cider* (EP Publishers, Wakefield, 1981)

Some useful addresses

The Museum of Cider, The Cider Mills, Ryeland Street, Hereford (0432–54207): the only specialist cider museum in the country. Closely linked to Bulmer's. Attractions include a shop, tastings, exhibits and a working cooper.

The Museum of English Rural Life, University of Reading, Berkshire (0734–85123), and The Welsh Folk Museum, St Fagan's, Cardiff, both have good displays of cider-making equipment.

The National Association of Cider Makers, Georgian House, Trinity Street, Dorchester, Dorset (0305–64086): can provide useful information about today's cider industry.

The Long Ashton Research Station, University of Bristol (027 580 2181): has done much work on apples and cider-making over the years. Its library contains many cider classics.

Index

Reader's Recommendations

Use this form to recommend any establishment selling
Traditional Draught Cider for consumption on or off the
premises. (BLOCK CAPITALS PLEASE)

To: David Mabey
    Good Cider
    Whittet Books Ltd
    113 Westbourne Grove
    London W2 4UP

Name of establishment _____

Address _____

_____

Telephone No. (if known) _____

Type of establishment (please tick) ☐ Pub ☐ Cider House
☐ Off-licence ☐ Shop ☐ Restaurant/wine bar

Date visited _____

Cider(s) sold. Please give maker *and* brand if possible.

1. _____

2. _____

3. _____

General comments _____

_____

_____

_____

_____

Name and address of sender _____

_____

COUNTRYMAN
MEDIUM DRY
SCRUMPY

MASTER CIDER MAKERS for MANY GENERATIONS

STILL FARM CIDER

Produced by

COUNTRYMAN CIDER
Felldownhead • Milton Abbot
Tavistock • Devon

CONTENTS 70CL.
TO BE CONSUMED WITHIN 48 HRS OF OPENING

POMMIA
SPARKLING CIDER
Made and Blended for
Roberts Scoones & Co. Ltd.
6 Snow Hill
London E C 1

Medium Sweet   750 ml 26.4 fl oz

TAUNTON
DRY
BLACKTHORN
CIDER

275 ml 9.7 fl oz
MADE BY THE TAUNTON CIDER CO. LTD. NORTON FITZWARREN · SOMERSET · ENGLAND

Churc...
CHURCHW...
CIDE...

Churchwards

| 1 Gallon | DEVON MIX **CIDER** | 4.55 Litres |

YALBERTON FARM. PAIGNTON 558157

1 litre   No Deposit

COATES
Triple Vintage

STRONG STILL CIDER
PRODUCED IN ENGLAND · R N COATE & CO. SHEPTON MALLET. SOMERSET.

Est. 1904
THATCHERS

Special Vintage Cider

SERVED CHILLED
Made & bottled at Myrtle Farm, Sandford, Bristol, Avon.
70cl

NO DEPOSIT
MATURED
W...

SYMONDS' CIDER & ENGLISH WINE CO.
Old Fashioned

SCRUMPY JACK
CIDER

RETURNABLE   Registered Brand

SYMONDS'
SCRUMPY
JACK Brand
Registered

Old Fashioned
made
Cider

TRADE MARK

ESTABLISHED 1727

Produced from Herefordshires' Famous Cider Orchards
SYMONDS' CIDER & ENGLISH WINE CO.
Cider & Perry Mills, Stoke Lacy, Herefordshire, England.

BY APPOINTMENT
CIDER...
WILLIAM GAYNER & SO...

GAY...
Norfo...
CY...
1

NO DEP...
PRODUCED IN ENGLAND—WILLIAM GA...